Shannon— my best to you!

# Each of Us

## *How Every Woman Can Earn More Money In Corporate America*

*Patricia Smith*

**Q1 Communicators, Inc.**
**Columbus, Ohio USA**

Published by
Q1 Communicators, Inc.
Columbus, Ohio

*Cover Design by Q.V. Design, Columbus, OH*

Library of Congress Catalog Card Number
98-91332

ISBN: 0-9655542-7-9

Printed and bound in the U.S.A.
1998

## *In gratitude:*

To my editor, Linda Belew, who pulled it over the finish line.

To my parents, Marion and Marjorie Smith, who taught me that each of us can make a difference.

To my husband, Scott Brooks, who never loses faith in me.

## *Dedication:*

This book is dedicated to those women who shared their stories, advice, inspiration and support; Ann, Annette, Barbara, Carol, Debbie, Diana, Donna, Elnora, Ingrid, Joyce, Kathy, Kris, Leah, Leslie, Lisa, Lissa, Maggie, Marcia, Marie, Marilyn, Meredith, Michelle, Nancy, Sandy, Shirley, Sue, Wilda, and to women everywhere. May each of us be everything we can be.

## *With Love:*

To Jesse, Ray and Rocky

The stories in this book are accurate, the names are not.

# *Contents*

> ***"The majority of women work in a small number of occupations, particularly in occupations in which the workers are predominantly women. Men work primarily in occupations that are predominantly male, although the number of occupations is larger."[1]***

CHAPTER 1

# Regular Women

The door has been unlocked. Business executives are waiting for women to turn the knob, open the door, and enter. Many women are doing just that. The majority of us, however, are still outside. We're waiting for someone to open the door, take us by the hand, and lead us through. When it doesn't work that way, we decide we are unqualified, and accept the corresponding pay level.

In many industrialized countries, business executives divide their female applicants into two groups, career girls and regular girls. *Career girls* are trained for management and decision-making positions. They are promoted and paid accordingly. *Regular girls*, also called office ladies, are cor-

---

1. Reskin, Barbara F. and Hartmann, Heidi I., editors, Committee on Women's Employment and Related Social Issues, Commission on Behavioral and Social Sciences and Education, National Research Council. (1986). *Women's Work, Men's Work; Sex Segregation on the Job* (p. 1). Washington, D.C.: National Academy Press.

ralled into low-paying jobs as they await marriage and family. This convenient classification method allows executives to utilize the talents of their female workforce without spending any more money than necessary.

This practice may sound shocking to us in the land of equal opportunity, but I believe the phenomenon is alive and well in the United States. Frequently called the “Mommy Track,” it is not blatantly advertised. We have more female role models in visible professions than ever before, yet they are still a small minority in a work force that is over 40 percent female. Most women in this country still do the jobs of “regular girls,” regardless of our potential.

Not only do many businessmen view women as either career women or regular women-we do it to ourselves. We work year after year, just like the men around us, without changing the way we see ourselves. Right now you probably know which category you fit. Regardless of whether or not you currently work, how long you have worked, or even the kind of work you do, you probably cannot shake your perception of which group you belong to. You are either a regular woman or a career woman. This self-imposed classification, more than anything else *you* do, will define your income during your lifetime.

We stick to this classification, believing we must choose between our careers and our personal lives. We believe our work is something we do *against* our families, while the men around us believe they are working *for* their families. We may believe we are not qualified technically to play the male games, or maybe we don’t want to “sell out” and become career women. Meanwhile, the men around us simply move forward, unburdened by these stereotypes and decisions we impose upon ourselves.

Others of us consider ourselves career women because we are in management. We have moved along in our career path and now supervise a group of women. We take our work very seriously, unaware that we are perceived as regular women by male executives, because we are surrounded by females, and our jobs are considered expenses. Our pay remains much lower than that of men at our same corporate level. Our opportunities are much more limited.

I suggest that you can and should pull yourself out of these classifications altogether. You are yourself, unique and unlike any other human who has ever lived. Your approach to work, your commitment to your career, and the skills you offer are unique. You can succeed at your work without any such classification. Without it, you can enjoy opportunities and income that currently seem beyond your reach. Without it, you can be free to develop new potential.

## *Men's and Women's Work*

Another classification in the business world is that of male and female jobs. While we can point to exceptions, there are still many jobs and entire career paths that are considered "female," while others are considered "male." Women can be promoted several times and still remain in a female job track. Some fields are considered better opportunities for women than others, but male and female career paths exist in every field and nearly every company. Almost always, men and women who follow male career paths in private industry will make considerably more money than those who follow female career paths. Over the course of a lifetime, the difference in pay is staggering.

Many women who work in low-paying positions recognize that they have fewer opportunities than the men and higher-paid women around them, yet they believe the cause is their own lack of ambition or qualifications. They think "male" careers are reserved for men and career women. Other women assume that the women's movement has made its mark, and so they will receive the same opportunities as equally qualified men around them. Many businessmen believe they give their female employees opportunities to achieve that rival, or even surpass those for men. Yet, the great majority of women are clustered into female job tracks, on their way up an entirely different corporate ladder than a man would follow and heading to much lower financial reward. Many working women and men fail to understand why this trend persists, in spite of the infinite talent women are bringing to the job market. Exploring the reasons for this, and how to rise above them is the subject of this book.

Many people are aware of the discrepancies between men and women in this country. We can cite study after study indicating that men far outnumber women in lucrative positions and that women often receive lower pay for the same work as men. All this is due to age-old sexism, for which there is no simple cure. But sexism takes many forms. If the executives of an organization agree to prevent women from holding decision-making positions, and to allocate the overwhelming majority of their payroll to men, this is a clear example of sexism. A more subtle example is a woman who feels insecure about her abilities or has never learned the unspoken rules of business, and therefore is unable to "play the game" by the rules, limiting her own possibilities. This form of sexism is probably more lethal because it is less obvious, and neither she nor her employer understand it. It is this form of sexism that I will address, the form that is within our control.

I am not suggesting that it is all our fault as women or that we should shoulder the blame. I propose that there is something we can do about it, and that we should. All women are raised with some degree of female training, which serves us well in many aspects of our lives. It serves us well in the workplace as long as we are surrounded by women, but it is not appropriate when we work with men. However, as long as you are surrounded by women, your pay will almost assuredly be lower than if you work alongside men. The high-paid women around you have learned what is more appropriate and applied it. They have either decided they are career women, or decided to let others think they are.

It has always been tough to stay in business and make a profit, and it is more so now. Fax machines move written information faster than the mail, or even express delivery. Computers supply us instantly with information that used to take weeks to collect. The internet can put information in the hands of millions simultaneously. Customers expect more, and they get more from the competition, both domestically and abroad. Sharp, savvy, knowledgeable people are needed like never before. Corporations in this country simply cannot afford to underemploy half their work force. Many employers are beginning to realize the potential that exists within their female ranks. Executives who are in a position to promote women's careers expect us to behave in certain ways on the job. They don't always understand why we act and react the way we do, and they don't have time to analyze it. They don't have time to train us to be career women. We need to make these changes ourselves; and we can. We are women. We are the most accommodating group of people on earth. It is time to make some accommodations for our own good. A few adaptations in our methods can change our careers.

So what are the options? We could continue to support the men around us, making their jobs easier, making them look good, helping them earn more, as most of us currently do. This cheerleading role comes naturally to many of us. Some are convinced it will lead to the job of quarterback. Others have decided that the playing field is a deadly place, and the sidelines are safer. But we have trouble paying our bills from where we are.

We could stand on the sidelines and scream "Unfair! Unfair!" even in large numbers. This may result in a few more women being "allowed" to play, much to the resentment of the rest of the team.

I propose that we learn the rules, with all their inconsistencies and nonsense, run onto the field, and join the game.

If we want to make the money associated with "men's jobs," *we need to do the work that they do.* This is not as difficult or as frightening as some women may think. It does not require a transformation of personality or ethics. It, however, requires some awareness.

## *Change Lanes*

The best and easiest way to ensure that you will earn more is to move into a male career path and stay there. Try to stop thinking of is as changing levels or having higher ambitions. It is a change to a different job, but not necessarily a harder or more stressful job. Move out of the slow lane and into the passing lane. Even if you are never promoted again, you will almost certainly make much more money in your lifetime than if you stay in a female career path.

Maybe you were hoping I could teach you how to keep your current job and get paid what you think you are worth. If I had that formula, I would certainly share it with you. Aside from some tips on asking for a raise, however, there is little I can offer you. Female career paths are low-paying. You may want to learn how to convince your management that your position is just as crucial to the success of the company as others that pay more. You can try for the rest of your working life, but you will probably fail.

It may appear that male career paths pay better because they are occupied by men. That may be true, but management has its own set of reasons why they *believe* male career paths pay more money. Whether these reasons are valid does not matter. Whether the rules make sense does not matter. If you want to make more money, the most assured way is to *do the jobs that pay more*. You are much more prepared to do this than you think.

I'm sorry to rip you away from a career you may love, but I know there are other jobs out there that you can love equally well. There are jobs that can be just as challenging and rewarding, utilize your unique skills, and pay you twice, three times, or ten times what you currently earn. After reading this book you can decide yourself whether you want to make a change.

Let's return to the premise that two classifications exist in the business world:

- Women are divided (by themselves and others) into two groups: career women or regular women.
- Male and female job tracks exist, and the male job tracks pay considerably better.

These are both oversimplified, but the premise can help us define why we are where we are and where we want to go. You can make both of these silly classifications work in your favor.

From this point forward, *forget about* classifying yourself as a regular woman or a career woman. Do not burden yourself with decisions about which classification you fit. Men have no such classification method. The jobs they perform are infinitely varied, and so are the ways they perceive their own commitment to their jobs and to work itself. The kind of work men want to do usually changes several times during a lifetime, as do the level of ambition they bring to the workforce and the sacrifices they are willing to make for work. To divide the entire male workforce into two categories would seem completely absurd, not to mention ineffective. It is equally absurd and ineffective to do so with women.

Even after you discard this classification for yourself, remember that others have not done so. You must appear and behave like a career woman to earn more for your efforts. So what? Maintain the image you need, and you can be free to be who you are. Use the unenlightened mindset of others to help you get the job you need to pay your bills.

If you are like most women, you see yourself as a regular woman, or at least on that side of the continuum. Examining the reasons *why* may help you overcome any need to classify yourself. I believe there are three reasons why women do not categorize themselves as career women.

1. They believe they lack sufficient ambition.
2. They see the sacrifices as too great.
3. They view themselves as unqualified.

## *Ambition*

Think about how you define the term ambition. You may believe that people either have it or they don't, and there is no middle ground. Many assume that if a woman wants a "man's job," then she must also aspire to be president of the company, or president of a larger company, or chairman of the board. If you have no desire to lead the company, or even lead the division, you may decide you are a regular woman and accept the corresponding pay. You may believe that at some future point you will have the necessary ambition, but that right now you should accept the lot of a regular woman.

Ambition, of course, is not an either-or concept. The majority of working men do not aspire to be president of the company for which they work, yet they expect to earn enough to support themselves. They do not worry about unbridled ambition ruining their lives. They know that business is not a conveyor belt that they get on and cannot control. People are not promoted against their will.

There are dangers to placing too much emphasis on ambition, or the lack of it. The issue of ambition may cloud your evaluation of a specific job opportunity. You may look at other people and decide what their level of ambition is, but you may be completely wrong. You may be wrong about your own ambition level, or you may be unsure of it. This uncertainty may seem to be an important obstacle to overcome. You may decide that a particular ambition level is necessary for a specific job, when other things are actually much more important.

You may not *want* to be ambitious. You might think it is unfeminine or unattractive to have ambition. You may be uncomfortable even talking about money and feel it is selfish and greedy to want to earn a lot. You may think it is somehow more noble to work hard for little pay than to work hard for a lot of pay. Maybe you don't see yourself as competitive, but you believe a competitive nature is important to ambition. Little girls are rarely encouraged or rewarded for being ambitious, and we do not feel good about it as women.

Try to put these bad feelings out of your mind. There is nothing inherently wrong with ambition. *Everyone* has some of it. Without it, you wouldn't be motivated to get out of bed in the morning. Don't worry about how much ambition you have. Ambition is a vague concept, defined by different people in various ways. You work for many reasons, and one of them is money. You could spend days analyzing your level of ambition (and some would have you do just that) and not be any closer to a higher paycheck. Spend your time instead on the other concepts presented in this publication, and try to forget about ambition. False perceptions and feeling bad about it can get in your way. And remember that the great majority of men around you are not giving their ambition a single thought.

## *Sacrifices*

Evaluate your definition of a *career woman* and the sacrifices she makes. Perhaps you believe she has few other priorities in her life, since her career dominates her schedule and her energies. She will pay almost any price to climb farther and earn more. She must travel for days or weeks at a time, often without notice. She must choose not to have a family or watch her family take a back seat to her career, causing irreparable damage to her relationships and her children. If this is the image you have, no wonder you are not anxious to join her.

The fact is, different jobs require different kinds of sacrifices. Consider this statement from my friend Shirley about her new job: "Now that I have a man's job, I work half as hard and get paid twice as much."

I don't want to discount the contribution men make to American business, but don't assume that higher paying jobs require any more sacrifice than you currently make. Whatever you do for a living, there are many men who work less hard and get paid more than you do. You probably know some of them. Yes, there are high-stress jobs that require long hours. Yes, there are career paths that demand a lot of travel. But many jobs that are normally held by men require far less sacrifice than you might imagine.

When we speak of sacrifice, let's not forget the sacrifice made by the low-paid mother who has four hours of work waiting for her at home, leaving no time to curl up and read to her child. *All* jobs require sacrifices. I am constantly amazed at the sacrifices women are willing to make in long hours, extra work, sexual harassment and belittling treatment, when their paychecks hardly warrant *any* sacrifice! Don't classify yourself as a regular woman just because you have other priorities in life.

Most women who earn high incomes have people to help them with at least some of the following: housecleaning, meal preparation, child care, laundry, ironing, shopping, and errands. This leaves them more time and energy for the real priorities. Don't forget that you are already making sacrifices, possibly much greater than those made by many career women you know.

My friend Paula works with several men on a sales team. These men are simply working people. Many would classify them as family men. Paula does the same job, works the same hours, and makes the same pay, yet others consider her as career oriented, ambitious, and even tough. Fortunately, she does not concern herself with their perception of her. She does her job and goes home to her family, just like the other women in her office. She just makes a lot more money.

## *Qualifications*

The issue of whether or not you are qualified for a male career is the subject of much of this book. It is probably more simple, and at the same time, more complex, than you thought. In fact, "qualified" means different things to different people, even when they are talking about the same position. Melia and Lyttle, authors of *Why Jenny Can't Lead*, explain that when those in a position to promote others talk about qualified, they usually mean "politically ept." Women, on the other hand, usually consider *qualified* to mean "technically competent." They often can't understand why unproductive, incapable people keep getting promoted around them. The fact is, they may be considered more politically ept.

Betty Harragan discussed the word qualified in 1980 in her famous book, *Games Mother Never Taught You.* She said the word is used constantly and indiscriminately and that it actually turns out to be a magic word like abracadabra. Most of us need only hear one comment that we may not be "qualified," before we back down, rather than question the definition of the word.

You may assume that your lack of qualifications comes from a lack of formal education or experience in specific duties. This is a common female misconception. All around you there are men and women who have no more education or experience and sacrifice no more for their career than you, yet they earn three times your income. You need to learn which "qualifications" are important and what behavior is standing in your way, and then adjust your style. You need to learn the rules of the game. Playing them is much easier after that.

## *Let's Talk About Skills*

Men and women love to think that women are less *skilled* than men. They believe it is this lack of skill that keeps women where they are. I have known so many women who were capable of doing "men's jobs" but never knew it. This issue frustrated me so much that I decided to write this book. What are these elusive skills that we lack and men possess? Where do we get them?

Phyllis Martin, author of *Martin's Magic Formula for Getting the Right Job*, lists the most common responses of top executives in any field when asked what skills and attributes they seek:

- a good command of the language
- a high energy level
- a grasp of important figures
- the ability to work in harmony with others
- respect for the bottom line
- integrity
- the ability to remain unflappable in an emergency
- a feel for the organization's problems
- the ability to perceive (as well as to solve) problems
- flexibility
- a respect for and grasp of new technology
- patience[2]

Yes, these are important skills in any job. Yet do you know any one individual who is strong in all these characteristics? Do you lack all these characteristics? Don't assume that other people have some exotic qualifications that you lack. We all possess some strengths and lack others. Millions of poorly paid women have many or all of the qualities in this list. They just keep thinking they need something else, but they don't. They *do* need to behave differently in some ways. They *do* need to make the jump to the other side.

The rules of business are old and well-entrenched. They are also *unwritten*. To oversimplify, men are raised to understand and play by certain rules of business, and women are raised to understand and play by a different set of rules. I use the word *play*, because in many ways, business is a game. Try to accept this, instead of resisting it. If you are currently in a female po-

---

2. Copyright ©1987 by Phyllis Martin
From MARTIN'S MAGIC FORMULA FOR GETTING THE RIGHT JOB By Phyllis Martin Reprinted by permission of St. Martin's Press Incorporated

sition, you are playing the game, too. You just happen to be working the concession stand, while the more highly paid people are on the playing field.

## *Playing the Wrong Game*

Women work very hard in the business world. Yet we are too often making efforts in the wrong direction. Harragan described our misguided efforts in terms of chess and checkers. Women play checkers without realizing they are in a chess tournament.

Working women are playing their best checkers, and if most of the people around them are women, their moves make sense. However, typically male careers require playing chess instead. Frequently women apply for these positions, or try to be considered for them, but they continue to play their best checkers. Working men can't figure out why these women keep making such confusing moves. Apparently, they are "unqualified."

Thousands of women are hired, trained, and promoted on the basis of gender, and they accept this from the initial interview. Some corporate executives profess that they want to put more women in key positions, but qualified women are difficult to find. Many an executive has lamented this predicament to me, "We really want to fill more decision-making positions with women, but it is so hard to find *qualified* women." My question is, where are all these qualified *men* coming from? The difference in these perceptions of qualified men and women has less to do with ability than with understanding and playing by the rules. Somehow, savvy men know the rules or are willing to learn them. Too many women assume that an entirely different set of rules applies to them and persist in playing accordingly. Or, we don't *like* the rules, so we refuse to play by them. When things don't go our way, we decide the whole thing is unfair. We stay on the sidelines, where things make more sense. We receive lousy pay.

When we feel unqualified for a job, we assume it is our lack of technical knowledge or experience at a specific skill that keeps us from it. The reality is that our approach to risk, our task orientation, our inability to recognize and participate in negotiations, and our lack of teamwork are keeping us "unqualified." Recognizing this reality is the first and most important step. We have all learned to change our approaches and reactions to many things as we have grown and matured. Change does not come automatically, but it is often very simple, once we recognize what we need to change. Now is the time to change your approach to your career. It may even be the time to change your career. You have almost nothing to lose, and a *whole lot* to gain. Many other women have changed careers for the better, so can you.

The generalizations in this book about the differences in approach between men and women are just that-*generalizations*, based on research and observation. Try not to get hung up deciding whether you agree with each and every generalization, but rather determine whether *you* would benefit by altering certain behaviors on the job. This book is written to help you fully contribute your strengths to the job and be paid accordingly. You won't fit all the stereotypes, but some things will ring true.

To gain consideration for a "male career path" and function effectively in it, we need to play by the prevailing rules. Both men and women are expected to know them coming in. But the rules also tend to change, depending on who is in charge. Women are more likely to feel uncomfortable with this. We want to have things spelled out for us. We want to be told exactly what to do and which yardstick will be used to measure our success. Melia and Lyttle believe that women want the security and assurance of rules, with firm guarantees that lead to success. If things don't work that way, we often persist in believing that they do. That attitude keeps us exactly where we are. We could try to change the entire structure of American business, but we will most certainly fail. Instead, we can get better at playing chess. There is not a businessman alive who is perfect at playing the business game. We do not have to become experts, we just have to get better.

There is no question that sex discrimination exists in the world of business. It is not my purpose to convince you otherwise. There is little that you can do single-handedly about the attitude of the people around you, but there is much you can do about yourself. Other women are making it work for them, in spite of the circumstances. So can you.

It may be time for you to get off the sidelines and onto the playing field. I suggest the following:

- Read this book.
- Forget about classifying yourself as a career woman or a regular woman. Get that monkey off your back.
- Make sure others see you as a career woman.
- Change your style of clothes.
- Find out what you are doing that is inappropriate to your new career goals. Start to work on your attitude and behavior.
- Look for a new job. Keep applying and interviewing until you are on the other side.

*"If we are to make use of the unmistakable opportunity awaiting us in the spheres of business, commerce, politics, and industry, we must first understand what shades our perceptions and determines our complex ideas."*[1]

CHAPTER 2

# What's Wrong?

Before we can fix the problem, we need to evaluate it. Once women decide to go for a position in the male court, most of us are unaware of what we are doing wrong. We are playing our best checkers at a chess tournament.

This chapter covers the most important differences between men and women in the business world and ways to overcome those things which hold us where we are. Understanding these differences can account for much of why we persist in making inappropriate moves. They are a result of a difference in training, and we can make adjustments or overcome them. While a lifetime of conditioning may seem like an impossible hurdle, it is not. Many men and women have overcome physical, emotional, mental, and financial handicaps to achieve what was important to them. Awareness is the first and most important step. The worst danger is staying where you are without knowing why you are there.

---

1. Melia, Jinx and Lyttle, Pauline. (1986). *Why Jenny Can't Lead* (p. 41). Grand Junction, CO: Operational Politics.

Celia Halas found that, time and again, her male and female patients did not understand each other. She offers a summary of seven ways in which adult women generally differ from adult men.

1. *Powerlessness.* Women feel less powerful than men. That feeling is reflected in their self-concepts and actions.
2. *Self-doubt.* Women doubt themselves more than men do. They are not raised, as men are, to trust themselves, take chances, negotiate differences, or stand up for themselves.
3. *Other-oriented.* Women place more emphasis upon others' opinions and acceptance than men do. They look to others for direction and fulfillment. This dependence upon others for their happiness increases their anxiety.
4. *Self-blame.* Most women experience inappropriate feelings of guilt. Self-blame commonly pervades their lives, lessening their self-acceptance, distorting their sense of responsibility, and causing them to be misunderstood.
5. *Fear.* Women experience fear differently from men. They are more immobilized by it than men are.
6. *Fantasy orientation.* Women have been brought up with unrealistic expectations of life and are disillusioned by the realities of adult life.
7. *Ambivalence.* Most women experience conflicting feelings about their sexuality, resulting in confusion, guilt, and a sense of pressure. Often these feelings surpass the potential for joy and fulfillment in sex and stand in the way of personal and work goals.[2]

---

2. Reprinted with the permission of Simon & Schuster from WHY CAN'T A WOMAN BE MORE LIKE A MAN? by Celia Halas. Copyright © 1981 by Celia M. Halas.

These differences come up time and again in writings that deal with women in the work force. We will discuss how these and other differences-task orientation, approach to team play, definition of competence, negotiating skills, risk avoidance, and appearance-affect the success or failure of women in the business world.

## *Powerlessness*

No matter what our age, we grew up with stories such as Cinderella, Snow White, and Rhaponzel. These stories feature females as the main character, but always as a helpless victim, waiting to be rescued by a strong, capable male (preferably a prince.) The men have all the adventure. Our heroine is captured, imprisoned, or exploited. This exploitation is too often done by another female, leaving the male hero image untarnished. The heroine's powerlessness is always rewarded in the end, when she is whisked away to live happily ever after. Of course, none of us really expect to live a fairy tale existence, but we often insist on expecting someone else to manage, or at least improve, our lives. When this doesn't happen, it is their fault, not our own. After all, we are powerless. However, we are also the ones who suffer.

Lynda Moore, in *Not as Far as You Think, The Realities of Working Women*, explains that women tend to believe their lives are governed by factors outside their control. They are more likely to believe others, such as a boss, husband, or family, control what happens to them. We are also much more likely than men to attribute our success to luck.

In fact, people who seem lucky are often the least likely to leave their lives to luck. Instead they take control of their circumstances as much as possible. Luck, or fate, plays a part in all our lives, but anyone who counts on luck rather than her own abilities will be disappointed. The same is true for those of us who count on someone else to manage our lives or careers. My friend Edna and her husband spent fifteen years planning and plotting his career. They discussed which people he should get to know better, who should learn of his achievements, what his next position should be. As he climbed the corporate ladder, she gladly went along for the ride. Then they divorced. Edna needed to return to the work force and didn't know where to begin. She told me, "I wish he had just once said, 'What would *you* like to do? What kinds of things interest *you*?" They planned his career, but did not plan hers. Now she recognizes that hers was ignored, when it, too, should have been planned. What she does not realize, however, is that it was not up to *him* to approach the subject. Her life and its planning are her own responsibility.

Sandy was hired to make telemarketing calls for a software firm. She was told that the job would lead to sales, which offered about four times her current pay. She did her job and learned a lot about the product line. After a couple of years, she had not been promoted. She told the sales director, whom she did not work for directly, that she wanted a job as a sales representative. He said she would be *considered* when a position opened. Months went by, and he received pressure from his management to hire people with sales experience. The sales director never heard from Sandy again. Although I urged her to see him and tell him why she would be good for the job, she sat back patiently. She did not want to be seen as "pushy," although I reminded her that she was applying for a job that required such behavior. Years have passed, and Sandy has never gotten the job for which she is qualified. She is behaving as if she is powerless in her career development, and she is.

Women are much more likely than men to behave the way we feel. When we feel powerless, we act powerless. This may seem obvious to you, since of course our feelings dictate our reactions. As you work more with men and career women, you will find they often behave the way they are expected to behave, *no matter how they feel.* It is our behavior that is judged, not our feelings. My personal contention is that very few men are actually handed power of any kind, they just assume it. When women assume power and authority, they get it, at least a lot more than other women. The next time you feel powerless, try acting as if you are empowered. You may be surprised at the results.

Perhaps you are relinquishing power to someone you believe is more capable of managing your career than you are. Maybe you want to be taken care of. According to the *Working Women's Report*:

> "There are no 'parents' in the business world; no strong protectors who know everything, no daddies or mommies who will praise us for our good deeds, or indulge our mistakes, or take care of us in return for our loyalty, or punish us when we have the temerity to branch out on our own. Our bosses are just people, and work for the same reasons we do."[3]

If we wait for someone else to push, prod, and force us along, we will have a very long wait.

Consider carefully the issue of powerlessness in your life. Many of us *want* to feel powerless. By having no power, we relinquish all responsibility to someone else. We cannot be held accountable when we have no control over our circumstances. No one can blame us when things don't go right because everything was beyond our control, beyond our power to change. If this is your attitude, you are destined for a sad and

---

3. Bryant, Gay, with Editors of Working Woman. (1980). The Working Woman Report: Succeeding in Business in the '80's (p. 176). New York: Simon & Schuster.

frustrating life. You *do* have power over your own attitude and behavior, and it may be time to make some changes.

## *Self-Doubt*

Anne Wilson Schaef, in *Women's Reality*, describes the sense of "innate inferiority" women feel, because we were born female. Different women feel this innate inferiority to different degrees. Many of us have internalized the belief that what we do, what we think, and what we say is less important than what a man does, thinks, or says. Perhaps we reject this intellectually but battle it emotionally. One of the ways this demonstrates itself is in the *volume* of talking which each sex does. Be leery that you may be automatically "giving the floor" to the men around you. Maybe this is not because you believe they have something more important to say, but merely out of habit. If you are working with men and you continually allow their ideas or requests to take precedence over yours, you will lose their respect and appear to have nothing worthwhile to offer. You will also lose your own respect, making you less effective.

Professors who have taught in both all-female and coeducational universities consistently report that female students are more outspoken, answer more questions, and debate more issues in class when no men are present. In classrooms with men, the women tend to be much more passive, yielding the floor to the male students. Studies have indicated that men interrupt one another, and interrupt women even more so, at an alarming rate. For whatever reason, when men and women are together, men do most of the talking. If you don't believe it, observe the conversation at the next dinner party. Sometimes women retreat to the kitchen just to get a word in edgewise.

If we are operating on such internal programming, we will be less able to make decisions, exert our authority, and plead our case. The men around us have no such conditioning. No one steps aside for them, They have to speak up and stand up for themselves. It doesn't occur to them that others are following different rules of order. Don't expect them to become enlightened.

Perhaps you allow the men around you to dominate situations because you assume they are more intelligent, or at least are more knowledgeable about the subject at hand. Sometimes they *are* more knowledgeable, but it is not a reflection of their gender. If you listen, you may often find that the person who says the most, knows the least.

David Schwartz, in The *Magic of Thinking Big*, explains that we make two errors with respect to intelligence: we underestimate our own brain power, and we overestimate the brain power of others.

This is a problem for both men and women, but women are often raised to believe that men somehow are more intelligent than they, especially at certain things. My friend Lilly raised three intelligent daughters, all of whom did well in school and life. When we were talking about women's opportunities, she looked at me and said, "You don't really think that a woman is as *smart* as a man, do you?" Here was an example of some programming that her three daughters had to rise above.

Halas' book describes our female "body of training" as one that calls for passivity and submission when faced with conflict. There is a generally held notion that men are superior to women, and therefore they will be probably right if we disagree with them. When we are questioned, we doubt ourselves and react even more passively. There is very little place for this in the business world.

Some women do not experience self-doubt but still appear submissive and passive because they believe that behavior is what is expected of them. We somehow think that achievement and leadership are in conflict with what society considers appropriate for us. When assertiveness, boldness, and negotiating are expected, we may give our best submissive, dependent, and accommodating behavior. I cannot tell you how unqualified we appear.

The behaviors we know so well may be rewarded in a female-dominated position. Those of us who work in those fields may perfect the ability to get along with others, work alone, not step on any toes, and do what we are told. This is what we have been taught to do in our "body of training," and, when working with women, this is what is usually expected. Therefore, we continue this behavior when we apply for other positions, or when we are surrounded by men. Again, we are playing checkers to the best of our ability when the rules of chess apply.

Being "nice" is taught much more emphatically to girls than to boys. This philosophy-*You be nice to me and I'll be nice to you and we can get a lot accomplished*-works with many women in female occupations. However, the men around you may be coming from an entirely different angle. When the people around us do not subscribe to this theory, we decide that either they are jerks or we are wrong.

Frequently, we don't offer what we can, because we think someone else must have thought of it already. Don't think that just because *you* know something or have thought of something, it must be obvious to everyone. We all have much to offer our employers, and we do an injustice to them and ourselves when we fail to give our best.

Many women severely lack of a sense entitlement, or the inherent belief that we *deserve* happiness and success. Some men (and women) have too much entitlement, causing them to be lazy and expecting the world to provide them a good living. But to truly qualify for something, we must believe we deserve it. This holds true for a business deal, a job, or a spouse. Only people who believe they are entitled to success, happiness, and peace can hope to attain them. If you don't believe you are entitled, try to evaluate why. Then try to see yourself as entitled, just as much as anyone else. A male employer once told me the women in his employ were much more successful than the men because the women worked harder. He attributed this to an overabundant sense of entitlement in the men, who expected to make high incomes. When he gave women the chance to earn a lot, they jumped in with both feet, and they didn't expect it to come easy. You will find your female body of training can sometimes work to your benefit.

## *One Upmanship*

According to Wilson Schaef, an assumption in the "white male system" is that two people cannot be equals. When two men meet, one must be superior and the other inferior. Women, on the other hand, tend to see one another as peers until proven otherwise. This offers one explanation of how men and women approach relationships differently. Since no other possibilities exist for some men, they will try to put others, including you, one-down, just so they will stay one-up.

When I first read this theory, I remembered numerous times when male colleagues, for no apparent reason, had tried to put me one-down. I had never recognized this lack of ability to envision a relationship as peers. How I wish I could have at least one of those episodes to live over, now that I understand what happened. Of course, we all know men who accept others as peers and have risen above this view of relationships. The next time a man in a business situation (or any situation) tries to put you one-down, remember that he may simply be attempting to stay one-up because he cannot perceive a relationship as peer. Meanwhile, of course, this behavior doesn't do much for our already shaky self-esteem.

## *Other-Oriented*

One day when I was in high school, all the girls were called to the auditorium, while the boys stayed in class. A male speaker told us about boy-girl relationships. The purpose was to learn how to say "no" to boys, and thus prevent pregnancy and keep our reputations intact. This was over 30 years ago, but I can still hear the speaker telling us that boys think about their girlfriends only once in a while – in between cars, sports, future plans, and friends. Girls, he explained, sit around and think about their boyfriends all day long. Even at the time, I thought it ironic that a man was telling us what we felt and thought.

Whatever the origin, women do seem to be much more centered on other people, focusing on their needs and wishes and seeking their approval. This serves us well in the home, where children are helpless and need the selfless attention of an adult. However, such preoccupation with the needs and desires of others often stands in the way of our business success, as well as our healthy self-concept. If we don't keep our view of the approval of others in the proper perspective, two things can happen. We can become ineffective and unproductive, as a result of trying too hard to please everyone. We can also become addicted to approval, even allowing others to give approval as the only reward for our efforts.

Melia and Lyttle describe how some women's overriding need for approval and the corresponding fear of disapproval differ from men's need for respect or admiration. Approval implies permission. We think we must have the approval, the permission of others simply to operate. We start at the bottom and seek approval by following the rules. Meanwhile, others are hired and promoted based on their ability to create more effective, new guidelines rather than to follow the old rules.

## *A Pat on the Back*

Men are seen for their potential. Women, on the other hand, are more often seen for our abilities in the job at hand. And why not? As long as we feel needed and appreciated, we stay in the same job indefinitely.

My friend Laura was a middle manager in a female job track at a large insurance company. She had been there 17 years and had worked her way into her current position. She was pretty fed up with office politics and the obvious discrimination against women in her firm. She was frustrated by the slow-moving process to get things accomplished. She was offered a job as office manager at a small insurance agency. The working conditions, pay, and recognition in the new position would seem to make the decision easy. She accepted the new position and resigned from her old one. The executives she worked for came to her with praise for her work, telling her how much she was needed in her current job and how much she would be giving up in job security. Their tactics worked. She decided not to make the move, but to keep her old job, even though the executives offered only approval – no promotion, no increase in pay. How many men in her shoes would make the same decision? How many executives would insult a man by trying to convince him to stay on, with no additional incentive? Unfortunately, this is the history of women in the work force, and we live up to our reputation all too often. We are so addicted to the approval of others that we make needless sacrifices to gain that approval. In the end, we often have nothing but a pat on the back.

Men and women in "men's jobs" do not perform their job simply for the approval of the boss, nor do they stay in a job for that reason. Instead, they use their skills and abilities as bargaining chips for another job or pay level. They may not cash in those chips every day, but they are less likely to be satisfied with an "atta boy." We must no longer be satisfied with an "atta boy" either.

## *Self-Blame*

I once watched a talk show host interviewing a working mother. The host said, "Tell us how you feel, tell us about the guilt." The assumption of guilt was so strong that it was incorporated into the question! Women have even been known to feel guilty about not feeling guilty. Guilt is a healthy emotion when it causes us to change our behavior from wrong to right. That is all it should be used for. Unnecessary guilt amounts to excess emotional baggage, which only serves to hinder our efforts. If there is no need, desire, or opportunity to change our behavior, we owe it to ourselves and the people around us to drop the guilt. Feeling guilty causes us to concentrate on our failures instead of our successes and prevents us from focusing on the job at hand.

A tendency to blame ourselves for what goes wrong may cause us to avoid business positions that put us in the spotlight. How obvious will our mistakes be when all the world knows our every action? The reason for this tendency may be our lack of confidence or our unrealistic view of "competency," which we will discuss later. Whatever the reason, self-blame has a very limited place in the business world. We have all read about business men and women who refuse to see anything wrong in evading income tax or cheating their customers. These people *should* blame themselves for their wrong actions. But we must not blame ourselves when we make honest mistakes on the job. We must be aware that everyone makes mistakes, and the most successful of us make the most.

When it comes to mistakes, we must train ourselves to see them as learning tools, rather than indicators of our lack of ability. Women are much more likely to overemphasize our mistakes. We regard them as proof that we were unprepared and unable to do our job. We see mistakes as failures, and we view failure as unforgivable.

The men and career women around us are making mistakes left and right and coming out kicking. So must we.

## *Fear*

What are we so afraid of? Each of us has a certain fear of the unknown, of stepping out of our "comfort zone." Yet nothing great has ever been achieved without taking that step. If you wait until you are comfortable with a challenging task, or until you believe that you can do it with no possibility of failure, it can never be great. Someone braver will do it and steal your thunder. I see women step out of their comfort zone all the time in other areas of their lives. None of us knows exactly what to expect when we have a baby, yet millions of women eagerly take on this unknown responsibility. The same woman who would be terrified to be a stockbroker enthusiastically leads a group of children and adults for a week of vacation Bible school, with no training or knowledge about how the program has been run in the past.

Susan has been a saleswoman for the past fifteen years. When she explains what she does for a living, women often ask, "You don't go out and *see* people, do you?" No man has ever asked her this question. Susan considers her job to be a lot of things, and scary is one of them. However, she refuses to let a little fear stand between her and a thrilling job with an excellent income.

Men, of course, experience fear of the unknown. Perhaps because working and supporting a family are so well ingrained as part of the male sense of responsibility, men often reach out beyond their comfort zone in the workplace, while women tend to do it at home and in volunteer work.

Larry and I were close friends. He was a banker, and he wanted to promote Jackie, a female teller, to loan officer, believing she would be an asset to the company in that position. When he approached her, he expected her to welcome the opportunity for advancement. Instead, Jackie spent weeks telling Larry of her insecurities. Could she handle it? Would she like it? What if she made a mistake? He discussed this with me, and I told him that women are unaware of the need to project confidence when they do not feel it. I explained that women want to feel *completely* competent in a job before they begin it. Taking my advice, he continued to encourage her. Without my coaching, Larry would have assumed that Jackie was not interested, and he would have looked elsewhere. Jackie would have been convinced it was because she was unqualified.

The men around you probably don't have a woman coaching them about their female employees. They will most likely interpret your expressions of fear and doubt as lack of interest or lack of "competence." It is all right to feel afraid about your ability to do a job, but it is usually counterproductive to express that feeling in the workplace.

How many of us don't want to interview for a job because we don't know all the right answers? How many of us don't apply for a lucrative position because we don't know every single thing that will be asked of us? It is high time to risk making some mistakes and some wrong decisions, even if we fall flat on our faces. Inaction in the face of unknowns is usually ill-advised in a business context. If you think you are not ready to do something new or you fear that you will make a mistake, do it anyway.

Many women are familiar with the fear of failure, or the fear of the unknown, and many of us believe we have overcome it in the business arena. We often underestimate the *fear of success*, however. Women are more likely than men to carry this burden, for several reasons. Perhaps we see success as unfeminine, or we view money as corrupting. We may think our lives will take a negative turn if we earn more money than our husbands. We may believe we will lose modesty and humility if we achieve what we define as success. These fears may not be overtly expressed, but they keep our incomes low. Martha Friedman discusses this phenomenon in *Overcoming the Fear of Success*. If we unconsciously feel we do not deserve something, we will make sure we do not achieve it. This fear of success resides mostly in the unconscious, and it causes us to sabotage our behavior. It can be overcome, however, or at least modified.

Try to examine your fears and your reasons for them. Then make a list of those times when you did something in spite of your fears and uncertainties, and what happened as a result. In business, we are rewarded more often for taking a chance than for being cautious.

What if you get fired? I believe the fear of being fired is more prevalent in women than in men. Highly successful people usually have at least one instance of being fired during their career. This is simply because they have been in high-risk or high-profile positions. When they failed to perform as expected, for whatever reason, they were fired. People who have been fired invariably report that they were devastated when it happened, but that the experience ultimately led to greater opportunities. The next time you hesitate to take a risk, ask yourself if you are afraid of being fired. Then picture yourself as fired. What would you do first? Second? By imagining what we consider to be the worst, we can often overcome the fear of that very thing. Besides, you almost certainly will not be fired. It seems to me the people with the least desirable jobs are the most afraid of losing them.

Perhaps you are afraid of your boss, simply because he or she is your boss. Because this fear of authority is very childlike, it eventually may cause your boss to see you as less than an adult. Remember that bosses are only people. They forget to take out the trash, just like we do, and they get scared and confused when things don't turn out the way they expected. Successfully carrying out the duties of your job is important in business, while cowering and shaking in the presence of your boss are not. Don't assume the people around you are not afraid, and don't let fear determine your behavior.

## *Price of Success*

Too often, women interpret criticism from others and minor setbacks at work as signs of failure. Success in business has its price. People may criticize you, and you may have to take full responsibility when things go wrong. I suggest that you can choose to view such criticism and setbacks as the price one pays for success, rather than an indication of failure. Plenty of men and women can take it, and so can you.

Try not to let fear immobilize you, and certainly do not wait until you have no fear. A common misconception about brave people is that they are not afraid. Nothing could be further from the truth. Brave people simply accept their fear, make positive use of the energy it provides, and try not to let it change their course.

## *Fantasies*

Believe it or not, women tend to expect more from their work environment than men do. Moore's book cites research that compares men's and women's expectations about work. Women tend to want pleasant working conditions, friendly coworkers, and supervisors we admire and respect. We want to be intellectually stimulated and respected by other people. Although men also want these things, they rate other factors as more important. In addition, the research showed that the longer men work, the more realistic their expectations become about work. In contrast, the women in the study remained idealistic. Our expectations are higher than those of men, but so are the chances of being disappointed. I found this study fascinating in light of what women as a group have settled for in the workplace. I suggest that women's expectations are fantasies.

Another common fantasy about work is women's perception that bosses should reward and take care of good employees. Men are much more likely to assume that good employees demonstrate an ability to take care of themselves, rather than depend on their bosses.

I believe these fantasies cause women to fool themselves in the work force. We cling to the notion that if we just do our jobs well, we will be rewarded. These fantasies – along with our tendency to do the job *too* well, sacrificing expediency for perfection, and our need to know exactly what is expected, rather than take a chance and try something new – prevent many of us from ever getting promoted.

Statistically, a woman is likely to stay in the same position longer than a man. She waits patiently for others to recognize and reward her efforts. She perfects her skills in one area before daring to try something new. She relinquishes the power over her own career to others. The men and career women around her decide when they are ready to move on, regardless of their level of perfection. They tell their boss when they want more responsibility, when they expect a raise, and why. When they are not promoted, they change companies. We assume that we should wait, and all will be well. Our managers assume that we are not interested or not qualified. Harragan claims that management automatically labels anyone who stays in the same job for many years as "unpromotable." How different this is from our perception that patience and perfection will pay off.

We believe the office should be a fair place to operate, free of political undertones. When we find it otherwise, we decide that things are not being run as they should, and we don't like it. We want to take our ball and go home. We can't give up the income, so we just find someone to commiserate with. We never make good money.

This phenomenon has gone on so long that men are much more likely to be seen for their potential, while women are seen for their ability to do the job at hand. Women see themselves for their potential to do the job at hand, ignoring the possibility of their next step, believing that someone else will take care of that. We want to be measured on how hard we work, what long hours we work, and how accurate our work is. In addition, we don't want to have to point these strengths out to others. Our reputation should speak for itself. Meantime, someone else has determined the power structure and demonstrated the true qualifications for the promotion to the appropriate people. We lose the chance, and we don't understand how such an illogical decision could be made. We change companies and repeat our behavior, or we stay where we are and wait for the game to be played fairly. None of this increases our income.

Our problem is that we see any adaptation as wrong, or even evil. We don't want our fantasy bubble to burst. If we hang around long enough, everything will be done the way we want it to. We are paying a very high price for this attitude.

I believe that women must accept the business environment the way it is and adapt ourselves to work within it. If your work environment requires you to sacrifice your ethics or sleep with the boss, then you need to change companies. But if your work requires the adjustments discussed in this book, you can make those changes and hold your head high. Many, many women have adjusted their attitudes and behaviors to further their careers. So can you.

## *Ambivalence*

Halas discusses women's ambivalence about their sexuality. In this book, we will address women's ambivalence about their careers.

Many women enter the work force with ambivalence. Before we even begin a career, we anticipate that it may be interrupted by child-rearing responsibilities. This dilemma is seldom shared by men. Parents, in-laws, friends, and others feel free to pressure young women about such issues as having children and making career decisions after children are born. No wonder, then, that women are ambivalent, feeling pulled in all directions. Typically, men see work as something they do *for* their family, while we see it as something we do *against* our family's best interests. If you compete with a man for a "male job," you may feel this conflict about work, but it's likely he will not.

Some women reach adulthood before it occurs to us that we might spend the majority of our lives in the work force. We might have received training for a particular career or job, but we didn't take it very seriously. Now we find that we need to work, for a combination of reasons. Our work has become an integral part of who we are and how we see ourselves. It has given us a direction and purpose that we didn't expect. While we know we will continue to work, we may drag along traces of this ambivalence from the past.

Ambivalence may result from an inaccurate definition of loyalty. We believe we are not committed to a company or a job if we do not have what we define as loyalty. Melia and Lyttle describe differences in male and female perceptions of loyalty. Women tend to operate with what the authors call "marriage loyalty." We will be loyal for ever and ever, as long as our conditions are met. Men tend to use "football loyalty." They will be loyal unconditionally, even unto death, but only today. Tomorrow the loyalty must be renegotiated.

If you adopt this male version of corporate loyalty, much of your ambivalence will disappear. In a job interview, no matter what is said, the interviewer expects you to be unconditionally loyal *today*. Forget about whether you are committed to work here – or anywhere – until retirement. Recognize that the men who interview for the job are committed to being loyal for *today*, and therefore are no more committed than you. Plan your career. Work your plan. If your plan is interrupted or changed, so what? You will still get farther, earn more, and have more options than if you stay in a female job track.

Your feelings about failure and success may cause you to be ambivalent. According to Moore, many women believe they don't have the right to succeed or to fail. By placing too much emphasis on our failures and too little on our successes, we believe we are entitled to neither and fear both. We adopt a crippling view of ourselves as imposters, fakes, and frauds. What a perfect prescription for remaining underemployed!

Look around you. All the career women around you were raised female, just as you were. All the men around you share your fears and uncertainties, to some extent. These people have decided to behave differently from the way they feel like behaving. They don't take the time to resolve all their internal conflicts. They act in spite of those conflicts, and they continue to evaluate what is appropriate behavior, no matter how they feel. So can you.

## *Task Orientation*

One of the most blatant differences in how men and women approach work is that more men tend to be results-oriented and more women tend to be task-oriented. Once understood, you can harness this difference to your advantage.

Simply put, task-oriented people take a job and immediately break it down into specific tasks. Then they complete the tasks, one by one. They are likely to make lists of things to do, and they take great pride in checking off the list. Although completing tasks is a part of work for everyone, task-oriented people tend to see the tasks as ends in themselves.

When asked to describe what they do at work, task-oriented people are likely to give a detailed explanation of activities. They measure each day by their ability to complete as many tasks as possible in a given time period.

Results-oriented people focus on the desired outcome. The number and nature of tasks involved are often unknown to these people. To results-oriented people, tasks take on three forms:

- The tasks that I must do
- The tasks that I can delegate to others
- The tasks that can be left undone or abbreviated without materially sacrificing the outcome

When asked what they do at work, results-oriented people are more likely to say they made an important decision or completed a report. The decision or the report might have included dozens of tasks, done by the person and others, but it is the outcome that matters to the results-oriented person.

One difference between "men's jobs" and "women's jobs" is that men's jobs are more likely to be results-oriented. The goal is defined: bring in $400,000 worth of new business this fiscal year; create an advertising campaign that increases sales of the product by 10 percent; increase productivity by 20 percent; reduce the rejection rate to 0.03 percent; maintain an inventory that minimizes overstock, but allows us to ship 90 percent of our orders within 3 days. The process for achieving these goals is at least partly undefined and must be authored by the person doing the job.

The kind of work that women do can usually be defined in terms of the tasks performed: type a report; change a bedpan; correct mistakes on an order form. Of course, men complete tasks and women make decisions, but you can observe this distinct difference in how our jobs are defined and measured.

To get to the other side of the camp, women must learn to live with these job descriptions, we must learn to work toward accomplishing goals. The completion of tasks is important, but not an end in itself. We must learn to design the job ourselves, to create the tasks that best lead us to our goal. This involves taking risks, trying things we may be unsure about, and making mistakes. We must learn to delegate tasks, abandon unworthy tasks, and present our accomplishments in terms of goal achievement, rather than completion of duties.

The skills of both results-oriented *and* task-oriented people are critically needed in the world of business. Generally speaking, however, the jobs and career paths that are task-oriented are lower paying.

You can use this to your advantage, if you can change your focus from tasks to results. Learn to reduce a goal to its various tasks and begin completing them. The results-oriented men around you may still be weighing different alternatives, discussing the end result. In this way, task orientation can be a bonus, as long as we do not lose sight of our goals and do not see the tasks as ends in themselves.

## *Team Play*

Teamwork is so foreign to many women in business that we are completely unaware it is happening around us. Yet the inability to play as a team member can squelch a career.

Boys who participate in team sports learn about cooperation, taking criticism, and making one another look good, no matter what their personal feelings about each other. They learn about winning, losing, and playing the next game. Because of the nature of team sports, they also learn how to make deals and accept trade-offs. They learn to be flexible and have backup plans. Many adult women have not participated in team sports, and many have not even watched team sports very often. It is time we recognize the importance of team play.

Ironically, the same women who are willing to work diligently year after year, with only a word of praise as reward, will often refuse to cooperate with someone who has hurt their feelings or made them angry. If you have a sense of team play, you put aside all personality conflicts when the job has to be done. Women do not understand how the men around them can "go to the wall" for other men they do not even like. Men learned this skill as boys on the ball diamond: personalities and friendships are unimportant when you're up to bat with the bases loaded. In business, we are expected to work in our colleagues' best interests, even if we don't like them, in the interest of the department or company as a whole. Women too often see it differently. We want to play with our friends. We want to shine on our own.

My friend Steve works with Clare in the advertising department of a corporation. They both wanted their department to be more responsive to the needs of the company and its customers. Bill, from the sales department, told Steve he needed a brochure on a rotation measurement product, and he wanted to get it out "as soon as possible" to impress a large customer and to remain competitive. Steve said, "Okay, we'll rearrange our schedules and get it written and printed within two weeks." When Steve told Clare, she said, "No way, I'm not jumping through hoops for those guys." Clare confided that since she was responsible for rotation measurement products, she thought that Bill should have come to her with the request. Because he didn't, she didn't want to cooperate. Clare has no sense of teamwork. Her behavior ignores the common goal of selling the product to the customer, and she stifles the accomplishment of that goal. She is seen by the men around her as petty and unable to play as a team member. She is seen as unqualified.

Often, women are unaware of the teamwork going on around us. We assume that others are operating as independently as are we. Such behavior is seen as confusing at best, and even dangerous, by the men who observe us. The people in a position to help us promote our careers want a team player on their team. They want a person who is willing to put individual differences aside and work toward a common result.

Awareness is the first, and often the biggest, step toward adjusting our behavior. Begin to see yourself as a member of a corporate team. See your division or work group as a team. Begin to see others as contributors to a common goal, rather than rivals you are measured against. Stop evaluating their personalities or their potential to be your friends. Start to see them as people you can work with – or around – to help advance the company's goals and ultimately your career.

## *Definition of Competence*

There is a fascinating difference between what women and men are likely to expect of themselves on the job. Women tend to be far more demanding in their expectations of themselves. Perhaps you share this definition of competence in your own work.

Moore describes the nagging feeling women have that "I should have done better," and believes it stems from the sense that women do not feel entitled to fail or err. Beyond that, we often have a completely unrealistic definition of competence. Competence requires perfectionism, expertise, and unassisted achievement. Anything less is simply unacceptable.

Women often think of competence as flawless performance. If we are competent, we must have our jobs down pat with no room for fluctuation or different levels of competence. Typically, the men around us do not hold themselves to this impossible standard. No wonder they feel so much more confident in their abilities.

In business, competence means getting the job done on time, *as well as is appropriate for the occasion*. It means excellence, but it does not always mean perfection. Competence also means working as part of a team, not single-handedly accomplishing the impossible. Competence means taking risks, sometimes making mistakes but then owning up to them, and moving forward.

If perfection is required, how can we succeed? We hang around the same position long after our male counterparts. We think, "As soon as I get this department the way I want it, I'll think about moving on. I haven't done as much as I want to do here." Those around us who do not suffer from this ailment will move onward and upward, earning several times our income. We watch and wonder why management continues to reward shoddy, incomplete performance.

Women are likely to view our current position as a proving ground, rather than a training ground. Not only should we perfect our current job, we should somehow demonstrate the ability to do any job for which we aspire before we even apply for it.

Harragan writes that women believe a prerequisite for promotion is prior demonstration that they know all the work beforehand. She cites research indicating that men are likely to feel qualified if they possess 40% of the skills and knowledge required for the new position. Consider the difference between 40% and 100%!

Women who succeed in "men's jobs" have often learned to expect less from themselves, instead of more. They have learned to try new things when they were unsure of themselves, instead of waiting until they felt completely assured of success. They have learned to rely on others, rather than trying to accomplish goals alone. This might not have been a conscious learning process for other women, but it can be for you.

Let's say I am interviewing for a job. I believe that the job requires a flawless performance, which I must achieve all by myself. To feel qualified for the job, I must believe that I am capable of such a performance before I am hired. Is it any wonder that I feel insecure? Combine this with my tendency to behave exactly the way I feel, and I act insecure.

Now, suppose that a man applies for the same job. If he fits the description from the study Harragan mentioned, he believes that he is qualified if he can do 40% of the job. He also assumes that he will have a team of people around him to take up the slack and that he will learn the rest with experience. Sure, he has some doubts about his ability to do the job, but he knows better than to expose them.

Now picture yourself as the interviewer. Would you decide to hire the person who demonstrates confidence in doing the job or the person who seems uncertain about herself? You know that, no matter what my background or experience, I will have a hard time doing a job if I do not believe I can do it. This is business, and you do not have time to hold my hand and coax me along until I gain confidence. You will probably hire the person who believes he can do the job. You don't know that he sees the job as much easier than I see it. You don't know that he is masking all his insecurities while I am laying mine out for the world to see. As an interviewer, you don't know the reasoning behind our behavior, you only know your reaction to it. You hire the person who believes in himself. You know he has a much greater chance of success.

How do you view people you consider to be competent? Do you assign them superhuman characteristics? Are you disappointed when they make mistakes? What about your identification with your own achievements? Are you likely to think you have accomplished nothing if you have not single-handedly accomplished world peace?

What we consider to be good performance on the job may be impossible for any human. Until we can adjust our view of competency, we will never see ourselves as qualified for the jobs we so deserve. Until we can see ourselves as qualified, we will not be. Change your view of competency from perfection at all times to excellence in the context of the job. Make your demands on yourself more realistic, and you will be able to do more.

## *Negotiating Skills*

The art of negotiating what we have for what we want seems to be completely foreign to many women in the work force. Perhaps we were taught that it is not nice to expect anything in return for our efforts. Maybe we expect that if we do a good job, we will be recognized and rewarded automatically. Once we have the courage to make a request, we might refuse to compromise, when those around us are willing to give and take. In an arena where bartering and negotiating are expected, our lack of these skills bewilders the men around us. Apparently, we are unqualified.

As common as negotiating is, women often see it as a high-risk endeavor. In *Winning the Salary Game*, Sherry Chastain explains that a poor self image is evident when a woman sees negotiating as reckless risk-taking. Consider the irony. Negotiations are a normal part of business, and active players are expected to participate in negotiations. Women see negotiations as reckless risk-taking, so we avoid them. We have far more to risk, however, if we do not negotiate. By not negotiating, we appear rigid and uninterested – and, of course, unqualified.

We are often more trusting than men, more likely to assume that what we are told is the truth, and the whole truth. Conflict makes us feel bad. We are the peace-makers, hoping to make everyone feel comfortable and at ease. In a situation that requires conflict, we too often take things personally. When our request or suggestion is under attack, we feel that *we* are under attack.

In female-dominated job tracks, women often discuss their work and make joint decisions, usually without conflict or strategic force. As long as women work with other women, this method works. When we jump the tracks, however, we are suddenly expected to negotiate.

We must learn to recognize negotiating tactics, so we can see them for what they are. They are thrown at us constantly, from our management, our customers, and the men in our personal lives. We must learn to see negotiating tactics as a normal part of life, instead of untrue, unethical, and unfair.

Finally, we must learn to negotiate with the best of them. CHAPTER 7 will help you develop these skills.

## *Risk*

Why take risks? Generally, the greater the risk involved with a position or career, the greater the potential monetary reward. Terms such as "high risk-high reward" are commonly used in business settings.

Women too often retreat to what we consider "safe" jobs, where we perceive that we have less to lose. Unfortunately, we also have much less to gain.

People who put themselves "on the line," who are measured by how much business they generated, how much sales increased during their ad campaign, or how much costs were contained, risk their good favor and their jobs on a regular basis. They are also paid well. Those of us who support them, who are measured by the tasks we accomplish, or even our attendance record, will forever be lower paid.

Chastian believes people generally fall into two categories in how they view risk. Risk-takers think about what they might gain from taking a risk, while others think about what they might lose. A chasm exists between the two types. Risk-takers believe they are worth more, have higher aspirations, and usually end up with more of life's rewards.

While this may be a simplified view, let's say these two categories exist. In business, women are less likely to be risk-takers than men. People who are not risk-takers are quick to offer reasons why something cannot be done. Where change is needed for progress, and progress is needed to stay in business, people who talk about why things can't be done don't get ahead.

Over and over, risk-taking comes up in a business context. Results-oriented positions have an inherent risk because they involve so much leeway in their execution. We must learn to distinguish between calculated risks, such as making an educated investment in a stock, and risks over which we have no control, such as investing in a lottery ticket.

Melia and Lyttle propose that women might not understand why we should knowingly seek what we consider to be a dangerous mode of action when we can avoid it. We don't recognize that there is inherent risk in taking the initiative. Conversely, the man who does only his job, no matter how well he does it, lacks initiative.

Sam talked with me after his third week on a job with a new company. He had ordered something to be printed in a rush, not knowing that he would not get the chance to review it before the final printing. It was completed on time, but with a mistake, and it could not be used. The mistake cost his company an extra $4,100. Sam mentioned it in passing, annoyed with the situation, but not fearful. How many women could make a $4,100 mistake in their third week on the job without going into a panic? The fear of failure can cause a competent woman to do a poor job in a position that requires savvy and initiative and involves risk.

Good business people in key decision-making positions are more afraid of inaction than of failure. In a forward-thinking company, people are encouraged to take chances, try new things, and make a profit. This typically means they will make mistakes along the way.

At one company I watched a vice president, who had been with our company less than a year, make a big mistake. After some internal research, he decided to invest $3 million in a product that had been designed elsewhere. After the acquisition, he made the painful discovery that the product would not work for most people he had intended to sell it to. The product had a narrowly defined market, and it appeared to be saturated. Three million dollars, essentially down the drain. Sure, this vice president had some explaining to do. But he is now president of the company. He knew that it would be riskier to take no action than to make a mistake. To be vice president of sales meant taking risks. The results of any decision or action would be unknown. Maybe you don't aspire to be president of a company, but risk avoidance is deadly in any results-oriented position.

## *Appearance*

Like it or not, our appearance can make or break our chances in business. We too often look the part of our current job, rather than the position we seek. Believing that "when they promote me to vice-president, I'll wear $300 suits" can guarantee you will stay where you are.

You may think you go to work looking great, but it may not be the look you need. Think of the following adjectives: strong, competent, intelligent, and successful. Picture a few men and women who fit this description. Now add this one: sexy. Most of us, men and women alike, can see a successful businessman as sexy, but we have trouble thinking of a woman as both sexy and successful in business. Your husband or other specific men can probably see you as competent, successful, and sexy, but don't expect everyone around you to have this image. When women look or act sexy, we dilute our image as competent professionals. Unfortunately, many women who strive to look attractive are seen as trying to look sexy. Remember that your image in the eyes of others is more important than wearing what you like.

There is so much to say about the importance of appearance in the business world that I have devoted CHAPTER 4 to the topic. We may not like it, but our appearance affects our success. It is the easiest, fastest change you can make to be seen as a career woman. It is the *first* thing we should change on our journey toward a higher paycheck.

Much of this chapter deals with issues that have been a part of your entire upbringing. Business people are often told to trust their "gut reaction," but I suggest that women sometimes cannot trust their gut reaction in the business world. Our gut reaction is a product of our body of training, based on the rules of female order. You might be wondering how I can expect you to change your thinking and behavior patterns overnight, in an effort to play some game that you didn't even make up. Of course, we cannot change overnight, but we can and do learn to change. We all change through the years as a result of what we experience, read, hear, and say. Sometimes this is gradual, unconscious change. Other times it is more deliberate and conscious. Awareness is the first step. Once we can recognize that our behavior may not be appropriate for the occasion, we can begin to change it.

*"Each of us needs to define the woman we wish to be in order to communicate effectively in business and to be taken seriously. It is much easier to blame the other person—usually a man—for not treating us as professionals when without a doubt a good part of the responsibility for how we are seen belongs to us."*[1]

CHAPTER 3

# Take Me Seriously

It is time for everyone to take women more seriously. Being taken seriously simply means that people listen to you, believe you, respect you, and consider your ideas worthwhile. After generations of women being "protected," it is harder for a woman than for a man to be accepted as a bona fide adult. If the woman happens to speak in a high-pitched voice or is short, blond, or overweight, it is even harder. While there are some things we cannot or do not want to change, there are other changes that can help us get the clout we need.

The first step toward being taken more seriously is to take yourself more seriously. Begin to take yourself seriously on the job. View yourself as an adult. See yourself as a professional who has a lot to contribute to your company. View your time as valuable, your efforts as worthwhile. You may be

1. Chastain, Sherry. (1980) *Winning the Salary Game: Salary Negotiation for Women* (p. 114). New York: John Wiley & Sons.

doing this already. But too many of us go to work, do what we are told, and see the whole process as a meaningless exercise toward a meager paycheck. How we talk, behave, and dress determines how we are received. Unless our actions, words, and appearance are consistent, we will not be taken seriously.

If you want to be seen as a professional, start looking and acting like one. One mistake we often make is to use our place of employment as our only means of socializing. Our friends, our drinking buddies, our boyfriends can all be found within the confines of the office. Before long, we are valued for our friendliness more than for our work.

Try to keep this motto in mind: "I work here." In other words, "I don't come here for intimate friendship, emotional support, legal advice, or dating possibilities." Of course we interact with other people at work, but the motto *I work here* can help us be more productive everyday.

A healthy distance can help you maintain an aura of professionalism that you lose if everyone around you knows the intimate details of your private life. It also helps keep you out of the office gossip loop, a dangerous area at best. You do not want to keep the job you currently have. It is a stepping stone, a waiting zone, for better opportunities. The more ingrained you become in the office social circle, the harder it will be for you to break away.

Your days of *wait and be told* are over. You will be so busy executing the job at hand, setting career goals for yourself, and developing plans to work toward them, that you won't have time for socializing in the office.

## *Goal-Setting*

Successful people are the least likely to depend on luck. Begin to take your career seriously. Start planning your career. This may be difficult for those of us who are used to leaving the management of our careers to someone else. If you anticipate the interruption of your career, start planning as if that interruption will not happen. You can make adjustments when you need to. You don't have to plan each and every step until you retire. Begin by developing a plan to discover new areas of employment and then move into one. Determine how your current job fits into your plan, or if it fits at all. If it doesn't, plan how your next job can lead to your goal, and how to obtain that next job.

We can borrow from a common practice among financially independent people of writing down specific financial goals. Most high-income people have set goals for themselves, but the very rich have written down those goals.

Sit down today and write down your career goals for the next year and the next five years. Be specific. Write down the job you want. Write down the income you want. Now, put the paper where no one else will see it, but where you can take it out and look at it often. If you have a goal, you will find a way to reach it. Without any goals for our careers, we will flounder aimlessly. This may seem like a silly exercise, but just having a goal can provide the energy we need to move forward.

In addition to setting goals and striving toward them, we need to adjust our behavior and work within ourselves to gain credibility with others. In some ways, we need to think and act more like men. Some women may resist this: do we have to "become men" to compete with them? If anyone mistakes you for a man, let me know. Meanwhile, it is important to recognize how we may be standing in our own way, allowing our own behavior to sabotage our efforts.

## *Don't Get Hysterical Now...*

Women tend to use both sides of our brain interactively, causing us to use more emotions in our decisions than left-brained men. While we may see the innate advantages to this approach, "normal" tends to be defined as what most men do. In addition, we are more likely to base our self-image on the approval of others, and "take it personally" when our actions are criticized or misunderstood. Finally, there is a double standard when it comes to emotions demonstrated by men and women.

Some claim that women are not suitable for decision-making positions because we are so emotional. We may be seen as unstable. We are actually mistrusted. You have seen businessmen become angry, maybe even explosive, and people go on about their work. Women, however, *cannot* react in this way and hope to maintain the image they have worked so hard to gain.

We must learn to remove ourselves personally whenever possible. As working adults, we all have strengths, and areas we need to improve. If someone criticizes our work, that does not mean they are right, but they might be. It doesn't mean they don't like us, but they might not. We can all improve our job performance if we listen to those around us who criticize, suggest, or even attack us. A defensive, emotional attitude will not cause us to be seen as assertive women, but as hysterical girls.

A defensive reaction can allow someone else to manipulate us, also. If we become emotional or defensive about what someone has done or said, we will not use the same judgment we would use otherwise. As soon as people recognize this, they may use it against us. In business, it is always better to appear as unemotional and as logical as possible.

Women often express frustration (probably the most common emotion in the office) by crying. Men typically express frustration with anger. If you are used to working with women, you are probably used to tears now and then. No big deal with women, but a very big deal when working with men.

Jim, a sales manager for a magazine, told me that about half his sales force was now female. He was glad to have them on his team, but they "cried all the time." I suspected he had experienced one or two episodes, but it was more than he could handle. I asked him what he did about it, and he said that he tried to calm the women down, tried to get them to stop crying. I asked what his male subordinates did when they were frustrated with a situation. Predictably, he told me that they became angry. I asked him what he did about it. He said he just let them carry on until they got it out of their systems, and then the situation was discussed. Since his solution was obvious, I just looked at him. He said, "I've been trying to be their boyfriend instead of their boss." I said, "No, you've been trying to be their daddy."

Jim is not unique in his feeling about tears. Most men have no idea what to do when someone cries in a business setting. They see the person as out of control and unable to function as an adult. They may or may not hold it against you when it comes time for assignments or promotions, but don't take the chance. Don't cry in the office. Go to the restroom, the stairway, your office, the parking lot – *anyplace* – until you are calm. Once you have reacted to a few frustrating situations without tears, it will become easier.

If you want to approach an emotional subject at work, practice the conversation by yourself at home. Practice in front of a mirror, as many times as you need. This will prepare you to pull it off with a matter-of-fact attitude in the office. If the other person is emotionally involved, be prepared for a variety of reactions. Remember that the other person has not had the luxury of preparing a response.

If you are taken off guard and don't have a chance to rehearse a conversation, try to avoid showing any reaction until you calm down. A response such as, "I would like to think this through before I discuss it, please," is more acceptable than an emotional outburst. Expressions of anger may be commonplace in your office, but that does not mean you should explode. You may say things you would regret. Both men and women accept anger more readily if it comes from a man. Just because men are allowed to get angry, don't assume the same is true of you. I do not suggest you should accept whatever comes your way without an argument. You do need to stand up for yourself, but you need to be more logical and less emotional when doing so. If you are used to working with women, this may be an abrupt change.

## *Avoid Gossip*

It is a myth that women inherently gossip more than men, but gossip is often tolerated more in female-dominated professions than in male-dominated settings.

Judith recently changed jobs. In her previous position, she worked with a pool of women. Now she works with one woman and several men. One of her first observations was, "No one is hanging around gossiping. How refreshing."

Wherever you are, you can only be hurt by gossiping about other people's personal lives or job performance. Even if a statement is true, it is still gossip. Those who gossip often fail to see what they are doing as gossip, thinking they are just passing on valuable information. When you find yourself passing on negative comments about someone's personal life or job performance, you are gossiping.

Gossiping is petty and dangerous. One of the dangers is that you have no control over the way others will repeat what you say, or to whom. You can be fairly certain that others will quote you incorrectly and to the wrong people.

Beginning today, get out of the gossip habit. Stop yourself when you begin to talk about someone else. When the gossip begins, you have three options: change the subject, indicate your discomfort ("I'm very uncomfortable with this,") or leave. Once you stop talking about other people and stop complaining about your job, the people who like to gossip will stop coming to you with the latest scoop. Believe it or not, they will also talk about you less often.

## *Use Your Name*

A simple change to boost your image as an adult is to start using your name. Many women who have contact with the general public or with others in their industry never identify themselves. How can you expect someone to help you get ahead if they don't know your name? How can you expect people to take you seriously if you are nameless?

When you have a conversation on the phone or in person, volunteer your name. Whatever you do, give your first *and* last name. I am amazed at the number of women in business who seem to have no last name. Even when I ask for a last name, I am told, "Just ask for Debi." You may think this sounds friendly, but it also implies that you aren't important. It implies that your job isn't important. Every job is important, even though some don't pay as well as others. People no longer do business as Mr. Walker or Mrs. Jones, but they still use last names. If others want to forget your last name, let them, but don't you be the one to forget it.

In the context of our language, the word *woman* refers to a female adult. The term *girl* refers to a female child. If you think of yourself as a girl and refer to yourself as a girl, you are not allowing yourself to grow up. See yourself as an adult, and call yourself an adult. Yes, there are some people who are not offended by the use of the word *girl*, but many others are – men included. Don't use the word *lady* instead, and don't ever refer to someone as a *young lady* – it is a condescending term.

## *Image is Everything*

Image is so important I have devoted the entire next chapter to the topic. In the meantime, we will cover some issues of "attitude image."

Conducting yourself in a professional manner may mean that you have to stop making sexual innuendos and stop accepting them. You may have to stop kidding around about sex. You will have to stop flirting. Yes, men and women have sex together, but not in the office, and they don't have to discuss it in the office. You want others to see you as someone who has important things on her mind, not someone who is a good sport about a dirty joke. Being a prude may not be your style, but you can begin by not making comments yourself. You can usually walk away from such talk, or at least not laugh at what is said. You are trying to maintain a professional image, and you want to be taken seriously. You may have to leave a conversation. You are there to work, not win a popularity contest. Men can tell each other dirty jokes and still take each other seriously. It is much more difficult for them see consistency between a professional woman and a woman who jokes around about sex.

Note that the issue of sexual harassment will not be discussed in this book. It is alive in American business, it is a very serious problem, and there are many other publications that offer excellent advice.

Your voice says a lot about how you feel about yourself. Practice using your voice in different tones. If you speak loudly, can you do so without sounding squeaky?

Do not talk in baby talk. This may sound obvious, but I know grown women who sound as if they are in the second grade. Somewhere along the line, they were rewarded for childlike speech, perhaps by adoring parents or grandparents. They continue the practice as adults, at the expense of their image in the eyes of others.

No one likes a person who whines. If your voice or tone is whiny (we've all heard it,) work to change the way you talk. A slight change can often make a big difference. Use a tape recorder, and make a conscious effort to sound like someone you would enjoy listening to.

No matter how much you want to change your career, express a positive attitude about your present position. Whatever the circumstances, a bad attitude will cause you to appear, and actually be, ineffective. Do not complain about your job to your boss, your potential employer, or even to your coworkers. Regardless of how difficult, find the positives around you and try to concentrate on them.

## *Begin Within*

So far, we have considered outward changes that will help others take you more seriously. It is at least as important to start working on your attitude toward yourself. You probably have ways to pull yourself out of a mood slump or do things you don't feel like doing. The ability to project confidence and to build real confidence are within your grasp as well.

*Fake it until you make it.* This is a saying I learned long ago from a female sales manager. It simply means pretending you are competent, strong, and confident until you actually feel it. While it may seem dishonest, successful people do it all the time. Capable women so often will avoid pursuing a better position or even turn one down because they believe they are not ready or able to do it well. Instead we watch a man take the job and plunge right in without holding his breath.

In the business world, people will probably not approach us with opportunities. In most cases, we have to pursue a position and convince someone we are qualified and capable. In some cases, we need to write a job description and then convince someone that we should fill it. This often takes more initiative and confidence than we have. Still, we want to project an aura of confidence. We might be scared to death, sure that we will fail, but projecting confidence can do two things for us. First, others will see us as being confident, which is crucial to our success. Second, projecting confidence will help us gain real confidence. Too often we believe more education, training, or experience will bring us more confidence. That might be true, but we don't have time for all that preparation. Besides, we all know well-educated, experienced people who doubt their every move.

Project confidence. Don't pretend you know everything in the world, just pretend you believe in yourself. Fake it until you make it, pretend you have all the confidence in the world, and you just might start believing in yourself.

There are other specific steps we can take to develop the confidence that will set us free. Natalie Shainess, in *Sweet Suffering*, suggests that we should start expecting respect. We should stop assuming that what others have to say is more vital or accurate than what we contribute. We may need to question ourselves less and begin to questions others more.

Everyone lacks confidence at one time or another. As you listen to others, try to make it a habit to ask yourself whether they are completely accurate or whether their points are the only important ones to consider. Get out of the habit of constantly questioning yourself. Instead, develop a habit of silently and sometimes verbally questioning others. You'll find there are more than two sides to every issue.

No one has automatic self-confidence. Many psychologists believe that all confidence is acquired and developed. The people around you who appear to have the most confidence have developed it, refined it, and worked on it. So can you.

## *Empower Yourself*

Many times we wish to change our jobs, redirect our lives, or simply make more money, but we have a thousand excuses why it is impossible.

As discussed, women are more likely than men to feel powerless. We may not even be aware of having a list of excuses. We simply believe that the situation is beyond our control. Maybe we want the situation to be out of our control, so we won't have to feel responsible for our circumstances. Perhaps we understand the steps necessary to begin our change, but fear paralyzes us. What if I insult my boss by requesting a position in another department? What if I lose my job?

Try to analyze the extent of your excuses and do something – almost anything – toward your goal, and your fear will start to subside. We need to become more accustomed to working with fear, instead of waiting until fear is gone.

You cannot change your "body of training." Even changing your sex, something most of us do not wish to do, would not rid you of your female upbringing. However, each of us can change the environment in which our mind operates. No other individual or group of people can control your mind. It is this phenomenon that keeps prisoners-of-war sane and allows adults to rise above even the most horrendous experiences of childhood.

Choose what you "feed" your mind. All of us have self-doubt, but you can decide not to allow self-doubt to dominate your thinking. All of us can have healthy, image-building thoughts. Concentrate on them, build on them, and train your mind to react to new and more appropriate thinking.

## *They're Only Men*

The game of business follows the same rules that boys are taught, but men are not inherently better prepared for business in other ways. A major problem some women have to overcome is a deep-seated feeling of being inferior to men. When a man speaks, are you more likely to listen, than you are to a woman? When a man makes a request, are you more likely to comply? Try to evaluate how you feel about men and women and their intrinsic worth.

As you compete against men and work with men, you must believe in yourself and your own capabilities. It is helpful to remember that all of us, men and women, have strengths and weaknesses, good and bad traits.

Think about your perceptions of men. If you assume that all the men around you are more knowledgeable or capable, emotionally stronger, or more highly qualified than you, your view is simply inaccurate. On the other hand, if you see all men as shallow, one-sided, self-centered, and lazy, you will find it very difficult to interact with them effectively. Such deep-seated resentment may hold you back as much as feelings of inferiority. Get some professional help if necessary, but begin to see yourself as an equal with the opposite sex. It will benefit your social, personal, and professional life.

## *A Stronger You*

People who achieve great things are constantly overcoming barriers in their own minds. You may think you have so much on your mind already that you cannot afford to work on your attitude toward yourself. I suggest that you cannot afford not to. Begin within. When you begin to knock down the internal barriers to your own success, the external barriers will become infinitely easier to recognize and conquer.

According to Schwartz, belief in yourself will provide the energy, power, and skill to do things. When you believe you can do something, you will discover how to accomplish it.

Any athlete will tell you that the state of your mind can determine the outcome of an event. All the education and training in the world cannot overcome the wrong mind-set. Even if you have received a lot of meaningless, counterproductive training, you are in charge now.

Begin to alter your thoughts throughout the day. If you begin to change your thinking, you will also start to change your actions, and that will change the way others react to you. It is not impossible to decide what is on your mind. Consciously directing your thoughts can help give you a sense of control. That sense of control, in turn, can help you discover possibilities you can't see now. Never sell yourself short.

Too often we see a female position or a female job track as easier or requiring less planning. Actually, it often requires no plan on our part, since we leave the planning and management of our career to others. We somehow see shifting into a male-dominated job as a big step, a harder job to execute once we get it. Even if you do see it as a big plan, a big plan is usually no harder to implement than a small plan. Even if it is harder to execute, I'll bet you can do it. If not, change jobs again. Put yourself in charge of your career and life plans. Reduce your plan to a series of steps, and take that first step.

Several years ago, I worked alongside a woman who became my good friend, and we both had similar, results-oriented jobs. We found that we had very different approaches to our jobs. We knew each other well and depended on one another for a boost of self-confidence when necessary. One day, we decided to write down what we perceived to be the other's strengths, both personal and professional. Our list included things we admired about the other person, as well as traits that we thought the other should develop further. We now live thousands of miles apart, but I still get that list out and read it when I begin to doubt myself and my capabilities. I recommend you try something similar with someone you are close to and mutually admire.

Schwartz suggests that the number-one obstacle on the road to high-level success is a feeling that major accomplishments are beyond reach. This *number-one obstacle*, the feeling that accomplishment is beyond our reach, has held women back far too long. We see evidence all around us that accomplishment is not beyond the reach of other women. We must begin to believe it is within our reach, too.

Change the environment within your mind, and continue to change it. When you begin to see yourself in a new way, you may be surprised that others start to react to you in a new way. You probably will not be offered a new career as a result of this alone, but this alone can make or break any career you seek. Next, take a look at the environment around you.

## *Associate With the Best*

Surround yourself with people who believe in themselves, and they will accept your belief in your own success. If you surround yourself with people who are willing to settle for what they have, they will probably discourage you. They may even laugh at you. If you approached a female vice president of your corporation and told her you wanted to be a plant manager, I am certain she would not laugh. She would know that believing in yourself and your goal is the first ingredient in success.

You may think that you are surrounded by a certain type of person at work and can't change that, at least not in the short run. That is understandable, since none of us can completely control with whom we keep company. But we don't have to eat lunch with the same people we worked with all morning and will work with all afternoon. We don't have to engage in conversation that brings us down.

You may have to avoid certain people who make it difficult to keep a positive attitude. Sometimes, these people discourage everyone around them in an effort to unload and feel better themselves. Stay away from people who constantly complain about work conditions or management.

Laura is a sales manager who likes to say, "Hitch your wagon to a star," meaning that we should associate ourselves with and emulate those who are successful. There is nothing more conducive to your professional development than to have one or two women around whom you admire. If you do not find yourself in these circumstances, find someone you admire who works for another firm, or find a man you would like to be more like professionally. There are professional organizations in every city. Professional business women meet together by industry, by profession, and just meet together. Find some groups that apply, and join them. Then attend any and all meetings that you think are worth your time or you believe are helping you toward your career or personal goals. Get to know some women who are doing what you would like to do. I have heard that successful people leave clues. Try to pick up as many clues, and as much emotional support as you can.

As you begin to plan a career change and work your plan, do not discuss your ideas with anyone at work. For one thing, people talk, and you don't want your boss to hear anything you don't want her to know. For another thing, the people around you may well discourage you. They may still see accomplishment as beyond their reach, or they may be jealous of anyone who makes more money.

## *Life is Risk and Problems*

Remember, women are more likely than men to be paralyzed by the prospect of the unknown. Your reaction to change may not be appropriate, it may be a result of your female body of training. It may be time to discard old reactions. Because of our tendency toward perfection, we may want to wait until there are no obstacles between ourselves and success – but we will be buried first. We must assess the risks involved, eliminate as many as possible, and plunge forward into the unknown. We must expect problems, frustrations, and obstacles. They are much easier to contend with when expected. The frustrations you experience may not be failures, but simply the price of success.

Some women give up as soon as someone stands in their way, especially if that person is an authority figure or someone who they care about deeply. Just because your mother doesn't want you to be a corporate tycoon is no reason why you should give up on a new career. Your mother is not trying to live on your salary.

OK, so you are learning to see yourself in a new light, someone with control over her own life and with tremendous possibilities. You are working on your environment, trying to associate with those who can build you up, instead of pulling you down. Now what? Take a look in the mirror.

*"...executives say a good appearance coupled with (an) air of confidence can add thousands of dollars to your income."[1]*

CHAPTER 4

# It's All In The Presentation

Most women can demonstrate competence in their jobs until the cows come home without ever earning much money. Unfortunately, competence alone will not get us where we want to go. We need to present ourselves well and have the right people recognize our potential. We resist this, believing that our good deeds should speak for themselves and how we look or behave is secondary to the job we do. Too often, no one notices the job we do.

A group of successful business women, interviewed 15 years after graduating from Harvard Business School, report that image is very important to their success. They certainly have the ultimate education, what many of us consider the key to success. If these women think they need to have the right image, think how badly the rest of us need it.

Like it or not, our appearance has a great deal to do with how others perceive us. People get a first impression based solely on our appearance, they continue to draw conclusions about us on that basis. Others must see you as a career woman before you can qualify for the male-dominated jobs and be paid well. You will be amazed at the difference a change in appearance can make.

---

1. Chastain, Sherry. (1980) *Winning the Salary Game: Salary Negotiation for Women* (pp. 115-116). New York: John Wiley & Sons.

How you are perceived will make a difference in how seriously you are taken and how your requests are handled. No matter how competent you are or how good you are at negotiations, you will not be perceived that way unless your appearance matches your skills.

The trick is to project competence, which leads to the opportunity to gain experience. You will probably have to fake confidence from time to time. But dressing the part will automatically be interpreted as projecting confidence, no matter how you feel underneath. While our manners, voice, teeth, and weight matter, nothing makes as much difference as our clothing.

## *The Clothes Make the Woman*

None of us wants to be told what to wear. It goes against our sense of individual freedom. We want our work to speak for itself, and we want to be judged on our attributes. We want to wear what we like, not what someone else expects us to. While the concept may be difficult to swallow, dressing correctly can make a bigger difference than any other single thing we do. It should be the first thing you change. When you go to work tomorrow, try dressing differently from the way you did today. If you do, your image in the eyes of others will begin to change immediately. The people who meet you after you change your attire will have entirely different opinions of you and your abilities from those who know you now.

Dressing *in uniform* is more important for women than for the men around us. This concept means that people will not take special notice of what you wear. The purpose of business dress is to allow others to get beyond your clothing and recognize how well you get the job done.

So, what do you wear? While the range of acceptable women's business attire has expanded some in recent years, I suggest you follow tried-and-true guidelines adapted from John Molloy's *Dress for Success* series. This is not an area in which to take risks.

- Wear a tailored, conservative business suit, with matching jacket and skirt. Acceptable colors are navy, black, and charcoal gray. Your suits should have a classic style. In other words, they should be in style at least five years. I routinely wear suits that are 10 years old. Pinstripe suits are fine, especially if the stripe is no wider than a pencil and is not noticeable from a distance. Any plaid or herringbone should be muted. From a distance your suit should look like a solid color. The skirt length may fluctuate with style, but the hemline should always be below your knees. A slit in the skirt is acceptable only if it still allows you to walk comfortably and does not come halfway up your thigh. The jacket should not accentuate your bust, nor should it be pinched in at the waist. Fine fabrics such as wool gabardine or linen are best. Shiny synthetic fabrics are a *no-no.* Unfortunately, if you can wash it, it isn't going to look professional enough. You usually only need your suits dry-cleaned a couple of times a season. Try to buy skirts with pockets, which make for a handy place to put your hands when you are standing in conversation. The more pockets in a jacket, the better, since you will no longer be lugging a purse around with you.
- Slacks as part of a woman's suit seem to go in and out of style in various parts of the country. If your position requires constant bending, lifting, or running, slacks that match your jacket should be acceptable. Otherwise, slacks might harm your image. Never wear slacks to an interview.

- Your blouse can be slightly more inventive than the suit. Even executive men do not always wear plain white shirts. Blouses in various colors, worn with pearls, scarves, or a pin at the neckline will provide all the variety you need. No plunging necklines. Never wear a blouse that looks like lingerie under your jacket.
- A conservative lapel pin is a nice touch, but not necessary.
- For shoes, always choose low pumps or flats, usually black or navy. Your shoes should not allow any of your foot to show, like your toe or heel. High, spike heels will be sure to convince someone that you want to have sex at the first available opportunity with the nearest available male.
- Skin-colored hose are preferable. You should avoid black or patterned stockings.
- Your coat and outerwear should be tailored and professional.
- Keep jewelry to a minimum, and never wear dangling earrings. If jewelry looks like fun, don't wear it to the office.
- Perfume is not for the office.
- Short hair is better than long. Your hairdo should look about the same every day.
- I am always amazed at women who look entirely professional except that they carry around big purses. If you must take a purse to the office, put it in your desk when you arrive and do not take it out again that day. Put the things you must have – money, keys, lipstick, cigarettes, or anything else – in your pockets. When you go to lunch, leave your handbag behind. Do not carry a purse into an interview. Never go see a customer with a purse

or greet a customer in your office while carrying a purse. If you need more room than pockets allow, get a briefcase.

- If you have a casual dress code in your company, or dress casually on Friday's, you should still dress as above. However, if everyone around you, including the CEO, is in jeans and T-shirt, wear a tailored jacket over casual (not grubby) attire.

You may see successful women who do not always wear dark suits. Remember, they have made it, but you have not. Maybe these women would be enjoying even greater success with the correct wardrobe. Begin to see anything other than a dark business suit as potentially damaging to your image. Use clothing to your advantage, instead of wasting your energy overcoming the effects of your attire.

All this advice might make you sad. Maybe you enjoy wearing different kinds of clothes and jewelry, and you don't want to be that boring. Look at it this way. Not only will others see you differently, even you will be better able to forget about your appearance and concentrate on the job when you are dressed *in uniform*. When you make more money, you can buy jazzy clothes for all the social events, cruises, and other new things you can afford.

Many people think that business dress should simply come down to common sense. However, these same people are sometimes seen as slovenly by others who are in a position to promote their careers. Large corporations often have very detailed dress guidelines, especially for employees who are in contact with potential customers. Some guidelines are so specific that they dictate the appropriate watch bands and belt buckles for men. This is not an attempt to clone their employees, but an effort to improve the image of people determined to use only their common sense in choosing business attire.

Janice was a clerical worker who took a position in a firm where I worked. She was no smarter and had no more education than the other women, but she did not dress like they did. She always wore a dark suit and low pumps. In meetings I attended, the men I worked with always mentioned that Janice was efficient and capable. She had those qualities, but no more than many others. People saw her that way even before she proved herself. The men I worked with never mentioned her appearance, only her capabilities. She was there only a few months when a corporate attorney was hired, and she went to work for him. A few months later, she left the company to become an office manager for a firm in another part of the country. No one was surprised. It would have taken such an opportunity to keep Janice at our firm. Her image was not that of a "regular girl." Although she did not move into a male career path during the time I knew her, she had two promotions while other women, with more seniority, stood still. Her appearance alone made her stand out enough to allow her abilities to show. Interestingly enough, no one but I seemed to notice the way she dressed.

An argument that those around you don't dress according to these guidelines does not hold water. You want to stand out from them. You need to stand out if you want to change your career. And you need to change your career if you want to change your income level. Forget about how those around you dress. Forget about how you like to dress. Forget about what people say when you first change your image. Start to dress in navy, black, or charcoal business suits and plain pumps. You will be surprised at the difference it makes.

When surrounded by people in male job tracks who dress professionally, we do *not* want to stand out. Imagine this: you walk into a board room, where 10 people sit around a table. Nine people are dressed in dark suits and ties, and the tenth person is wearing a bright yellow dress. How seriously will this tenth person be taken? It depends much more on the mentality of those around her than on her contributions to the meeting. Don't depend on the mentality of those around you.

You may resist this because you don't want to play the game, because you think that dressing in business attire is giving in to "their" standards. I've got news for you. If you are in a female job, earning female wages, you are already playing their game. Look at your paycheck if you don't believe you have sold out.

You may be thinking you don't have the money to dress like a CEO. It is actually cheaper in the long run because you will wear the same clothes so often, and they will last many years. A good suit will last through hundreds of wearings. You are trying to look professional, not win a contest for the largest wardrobe. Try checking consignment shops in your area, where people sell good used clothes. From time to time, you may find something appropriate at a fraction of the cost. If you go to garage or yard sales, be sure to check the clothing racks, sometimes women sell their professional suits after having children and changing sizes. Instead of accepting all those silly gifts from your mother this Christmas, ask for a gift certificate at a professional woman's store.

You are not trying to look sexy. You are trying to look professional. Your chances of being taken seriously, being noticed for your abilities, and improving your career can hang on your back. The very *first* thing you should do to change your career and your income is to change the way you dress.

## *Mind Your Manners*

When we speak of manners, we often picture women sitting calmly with their hands in their laps, being *perfect little ladies.* This image will work against you in business, but so will mannerisms such as biting your nails, sniffing loudly, or applying makeup in public.

## *The Sound of Your Voice*

The tone of your voice and the phrases you use can make or break you. We have already cautioned against using baby talk. Some of us talk far too fast for most people to understand what we are saying. Some of us are in the habit of finishing other people's sentences for them, a habit that definitely annoys the speaker. Some of us don't know when to speak up, and some don't know when to shut up.

Think of how you end your sentences. Do you tend to end sentences with a phrase such as "you know" or "and all that" or "OK?" Just one of these can prevent others from perceiving you as an intelligent adult with something worthwhile to say. Also, be careful that you don't end a statement as if it were a question. If you seem to question your own argument, how can you expect others to take it seriously?

Educated or not, far too many people use poor grammar in their speech and writing. These mistakes can very quickly eliminate your chances for the career you seek. You notice it when someone violates a grammatical rule with which you are familiar. You can be sure that others are noticing the mistakes you make.

## *Good Dental Health*

Few of us think we have the perfect set of choppers, but yours may be standing in your way professionally. If you are missing a front tooth, replacing it should become a priority. Braces may be in order for protruding front teeth, but do not go to a lot of trouble and expense to have the ideal smile. Your goal is not beauty, but eliminating anything that detracts from people hearing what you have to say.

## *What Have You Got to Lose?*

Discrimination on the basis of weight is very unfortunate, but often a reality. Some overweight business women have reported being spoken to as children, as if their level of understanding were lower than those around them! Most of us in the land of plenty struggle to control weight all of our adult lives. The more weight we have to lose, the greater the challenge. There are organizations and publications to help people take off extra weight. In the meantime, or instead of losing weight, concentrate on presenting yourself in the most professional manner possible. Dress professionally, in suits that fit you now. Set your professional goals and work toward them, and don't let extra weight pull your confidence level down. It is your mind and energy that you offer your employer or potential employer, not your body. Throughout history, people have been known to rise above much more than extra weight in pursuit of fascinating careers.

## *Nose to the Grindstone*

You should stand out as a dedicated, serious, no-nonsense employee. We have said that "shining like a star" at your current position will not get you the career you seek. At the same time, it is very important to be excited about and dedicated to your current work. It can only hurt you if you are not. You cannot afford to become complacent or slovenly in your work performance. As you look to change your career direction, look at the company for which you currently work. Decide what you have to offer them. See what they have to offer you. It is important that influential people at your company think highly of you. If you leave the company, you may need a recommendation from your boss or others.

Janet Dight, in *Breaking the Secretary Barrier*, suggests we arrive at work just a few minutes early every day, not to make coffee, but to get a head start. We should stay at our desks after 12 noon and return just a few minutes early from lunch. This doesn't take too much time, and can establish your image as a serious employee. To some, it will look like you live there.

Anyone who refers to you as a "groveling" is probably not in a position to promote your career. Remember your motto: *I work here*. You can always find plenty of friends outside the company. It doesn't hurt to stand out as someone who is more dedicated than others. It might also begin to change your self-image on the job. If your ambitions do not match those of the women around you, why should you compare yourself to them? Try to be the one who stands out as dedicated.

If you have an opportunity to supervise other people for any period of time, take it. Do not pass up a chance to serve in a supervisory or management capacity, even if it is only temporary or your own work load will double. Too often women see things only in the short run. You might think, "More responsibility will bury me," when you should be thinking of your resume or your future with the company. Supervisory experience can only help you in the future, no matter what it does to you now.

## *You are a Subordinate, Not a Child*

Too many of us see ourselves as children when working with an authoritative adult boss, especially a male boss. Give the guy a break, he didn't hire you to have a child around. Learn to contribute by communicating with your employer on an adult-to-adult basis. Instead of simply doing exactly as you are told, speak up when you have suggestions – not complaints, but ideas about how to do things better. See yourself as equal to your boss. Remember that it's only your position – not you – that is subordinate to his position. You will be surprised how much more you have to offer.

Even if your boss does not have the authority or the inclination to help you further your career, that person usually has veto power over any opportunity you seek. It always behooves you to get along as well as possible with your manager. It also helps you to be more productive. Your boss might not be very good at getting along with you, so you may have to take the initiative to communicate better. So what? Things probably won't get worse, and they are likely to get better. Your boss might even learn something from you.

One other point about your boss. The line between manager and supervisor may be very clear-cut in your company, or it may be less distinct. No matter what the title, always refer to your boss as your manager, not your supervisor. Referring to your boss as a supervisor might diminish both you and your boss in the eyes of others. This may seem like a minor point, but people who work for supervisors carry less clout than those who work for managers.

Assume that every contact you make within your company or with a customer is someone who may help you succeed in your career. Be professional and helpful, and go beyond the call of duty when possible. I am constantly surprised at the number of people who have contact with the public and won't be helpful, even when it appears to be their job. Don't pass the buck, explaining that someone else screwed up. Just see if you can help. If a customer needs information that you do not have, promise to find it and call the person back. Then do it. Take responsibility. That is what having a real career is all about.

## *Stand Up Straight*

Watch the way you stand and walk. Good posture is one of the most significant ways to portray self-confidence. Try not to look at the floor as you walk. Look straight ahead. You might be surprised what you are able to see. Stand up tall and straight. If you are tall, all the better, since you are more likely to be taken seriously automatically. If you are short, there is no point in calling attention to it by slouching. Stand on your own, and don't act as if you need to lean against the closest stationary object for support.

## *Just What is Assertive?*

It is time to change the way you react to situations at work. You want others to perceive you as competent in your job and capable of handling a results-oriented position. Your reactions will help determine your reputation for working with others, whether others see you as cooperative, hard to get along with, assertive, bitchy. Remember not to take things personally. Begin to learn the difference between being aggressive and being assertive. Aggressive people verbally attack others and disregard their rights. Assertive people stand up for their own rights, but they don't attack.

You can always accomplish more with direct, assertive behavior than with aggressive behavior, no matter how the people around you behave. Being assertive requires standing up for yourself, without slamming the people around you. You need to stand up for yourself. No one else can be expected to stand up for you. As you negotiate for what you require, someone else will probably have to make a sacrifice. This is business. Don't think your company can meet everyone's needs simultaneously. If you knock yourself out to avoid hurting anyone's feelings, you will eventually lose the respect of those around you.

Some women believe the way to accomplish something is to be extremely sweet, following the saying, "You catch more flies with honey than with vinegar." This approach can come across as indirect, wishy-washy, and ineffective rather than assertive. Ask your close friends how you come across in various situations. They might help you see your behavior from a different perspective.

As you change your approach to situations, try to behave as a rational, assertive person who does not attack or counter-attack those around her. This is not always easy, when we are haunted with self-doubt or angered by a situation. However, it is necessary to our image and success.

## *What Are You Waiting For?*

Many women believe we should project an image of having patience. We think that if we are not patient, others will see us as pushy. Instead, we sabotage our efforts by hanging around waiting. We need to stop waiting to be chosen and invited to be promoted. We need to stop waiting to be told what to do and how to do it.

Too many of us are in a holding pattern at work. We see our careers as out of our hands. We're waiting for a fairy godmother to reward our efforts. Unless we make some changes, we will be here waiting until retirement.

## *The New You*

Begin to change your presentation of yourself. This is a step that you cannot overlook. Change your appearance. The purchase of two suits, navy and gray, will change your appearance completely. Be conscious of your speech patterns and use of grammar, both written and spoken. Do those things on the job that help you stand out as someone who is serious about her work. Work toward becoming more assertive, less aggressive, less accommodating, and less afraid. The benefits will last the rest of your working life.

*"Develop your communication skills. Few people can express themselves well, and one thing that separates those who move up from those who move sideways is the ability to say what you mean when you mean it."*[1]

CHAPTER 5

# I Know Business – or Do I?

As we apply for and accept "male jobs," we need to understand basic business concepts and be able to talk in those terms. The jobs we seek offer more than just a boost in income. They offer the chance to make a direct impact on the bottom line and see the big picture of how the company operates. To make the most of this opportunity, we must be able to converse with our colleagues.

It is certainly not true that women inherently understand less than men about business. However, our "female jobs" tend to focus our attention on the finite details of our tasks and rarely demand that we understand how a corporation operates. Far too few of us can read and understand a financial report. Some of us even see the pursuit of profit as somehow socially evil.

---

1. Wyse, Lois. (1983). *The Six Figure Woman and How to Be One* (p. 40). New York: Fawcett Crest, Ballantine Books.

To get the job done, we must understand what is going on around us. We must learn to focus on a result, whether it is revenue, profit, cost containment, or quality control. In addition, we need to understand the impact of our efforts on that result. Our best female training and all our female work experience seldom prepare us for this. We must prepare ourselves.

This chapter provides a brief description of some business terms and basic concepts. It is designed as a starting place, one that is hopefully easier and quicker to understand than several textbooks on economics, accounting, and finance. No doubt, you will gain additional knowledge on the job. You may want to attend specific workshops or courses after you change jobs. If you don't have much financial background, this chapter might seem confusing. Don't be intimidated. Read it a couple of times if you think it will help.

## *You're Not At Home*

Many a woman has lost credibility in the office by applying reasonable at-home financial rules to her company's operations. Corporate finance does not always operate like your household budget. It is not important that you know all the ins and outs of financial management, but it is necessary for you to remove your thinking from the way things are done at home. I offer a couple of examples.

I once worked for a firm that was almost a year behind in billing its new products. All new contracts were audited for mistakes. Because other priorities got in the way, the audits were a year behind. The customers who purchased the equipment had not kept track of whether it was billed and paid for, since that was the responsibility of their company's accounts payable department. The accounts payable staff had been taught not to call suppliers and beg for invoices. Customers' billing cycles passed, and the money was no longer available. When they finally received their bills, customers had to repeat the process of submitting the invoice and allocating the funds – hardly a process you want your customers to go through.

The women who processed these audits believed our customers would be happy to receive their bill a year late, since they had use of their money longer. These women persisted in applying at-home rules on the job, costing the company enormous amounts of money and damaging its reputation with customers.

As another example, housing is the single greatest expense for most families. Many find it is financially better to own a home than to rent. They can realize financial benefits each year by reducing their taxable income by the amount paid on interest, usually a sizable portion of the monthly mortgage payment. They can contribute a monthly amount toward owning. If they sell the house, they receive the equity built up through their own contributions as well as any increase in the value of the home. If they don't sell, at some point the mortgage is paid off and they can live in a home without a monthly payment to the bank.

In the corporate world, however, salaries and wages are usually the single greatest expense. Sometimes it makes sense to own a building for the same reasons we want to own a home, but often it makes more sense to lease a building. The needs of a growing company may change faster than the ability to sell and buy property. If you are a manufacturer, your needs for square footage and environmental considerations may change each time you introduce a new product line. If you tie up your cash buying a facility, then you might not have the capital to develop a new product line or acquire a competitor. If you spend all your resources on a building, you may not have the cash you need to get through some slow periods.

Theoretically, all decisions in business are based on what is financially best for the company in the long or short term. Even an extravagance such as fancy office furniture might be justified to impress potential clients or attract the right kind of employees. Too often, we think of office purchases in terms of what would make us happy, rather than what would make us more productive. The more we can think in financial terms, the more credibility we will have, and the more we can contribute at work.

## *Company Types*

Companies come in many different forms. There are three basic types of companies according to legal ownership and organization.

A **sole proprietorship** is legally owned by one individual. Any profit or loss belongs to that person. The individual may decide to have a key role in the organization or may choose others to manage all or part of the business.

A **partnership** is like a proprietorship except it is legally owned by two or more people. Partners may own varying percentages of the business. Profits and losses are shared accordingly. A **silent partner** is an individual who puts up money to fund a company or part of a company, but is not active in its daily management.

A **corporation** is a legal entity itself, and it may be **privately** or **publicly** owned. Ownership is divided into shares, and various people own different numbers of shares. When a corporation is publicly held, at least some of the shares can be purchased by whoever wants to buy them. Corporations usually have a president, a Chief Executive Officer (CEO), and perhaps several vice presidents. These executives may or may not be major stockholders. The CEO and president report to a board of directors.

Companies often begin as sole proprietorships or partnerships and then the owners decide to form a corporation. Many corporations begin as privately held, and later the shareholders may decide to "go public," or become publicly owned. These changes may or may not significantly affect employees. They do not necessarily reflect the amount of success the business is enjoying.

Do not make a career decision based on whether a company is a proprietorship, partnership, privately held corporation, or publicly held corporation. Examine the opportunity for you.

## *Industries*

**Industry** refers to a segment of our economy, such as the textile industry or the software industry. The industry is determined by the type of business a company engages in. Corporations are compared, and compare themselves, to others in the same industry. Your company may operate in several industries, or just one. Don't assume your company's managers know what is going on in the industry in which you operate. They may not, but they almost always think they do.

**Market** and **marketplace** are interchangeable terms referring to customers or prospective customers who might have a use for your product. Competing firms operate within the same market. Determining the exact size and makeup of a market is impossible, but successful companies try to learn as much as they can about their market for planning. The word *market* might also refer to the stock market, depending on the conversation.

**Marketable** refers to the saleability of a product or service. If you have marketable skills, you are able to sell your skills for a salary or fee. If a product is marketable, you should introduce it as soon as possible, to beat your competition to the punch.

**Market share** refers to a percentage of the total dollars generated in an industry in a given time frame. If your boss says, "We had 40 percent market share last year," that means your company got 40 percent of the total dollars spent on products of the same kind. In certain industries, such as dry cereal or fast food, increasing your market share by as little as one-half of one percent can mean millions of dollars. Market share does not appear on a financial statement for shareholders, but it is very important to many companies. In some cases, management follows market share more closely than the company's own sales revenue or profit. Often managers must explain to others in management as well as shareholders why the company has gained, lost, or maintained market share.

## *Line and Staff*

You need to recognize the distinction between line and staff jobs. **Line positions** are those jobs seen as making a direct contribution to the company's profits. Jobs directly involved in the design, manufacture, and sale of your product are line positions. Briefly put, production and sales jobs are line positions. **Staff positions** are those that support the line. Human resources, billing, and public relations are considered staff positions. Line people are seen as essential to the organization, while staff people are viewed as expenses. Line people, by the nature of their jobs, usually have more power than staff people. Almost without exception, line people are paid more.

One of the most blatant differences between the careers of women and men is that women typically spend their lives working in staff positions. Men more often move around between line and staff, and most line positions are held by men. This occurs partly because women do not recognize the difference and thus gravitate toward staff positions, erroneously believing them to be safer.

You know how hard you work. Perhaps the women around you remind themselves and each other how important they are to the company. However, staff positions are seen as costs. Women have many more choices than we used to. As we make choices concerning careers, we should know and understand this difference between line and staff. We need to land a position on the line.

I know of companies that have a line job in a staff department, when it was held by a woman. If you have such a job, you might want to approach your management about switching your job to a line position. "Clearly, my responsibilities are more closely tied to production than accounting." If you can get moved, talk to your new boss about a higher salary. You might also consider changing companies. It's possible that you could change companies, keep the same job title, and double your income.

Far too many of us choose staff positions to avoid the risk or visibility of a line position, doubting that we are capable of succeeding at a line job. The price we pay in lack of recognition, job security, advancement, and compensation does not warrant this choice.

## *Productivity*

**Productivity** is the output produced, considering both quantity and quality, relative to the investment of money, time, and effort. In business, productivity of individuals and departments should be measured as closely as is feasible. Too often workers rate themselves on effort expended or time spent, rather than productivity. We all know what it is like to have a hectic, busy, unproductive day. In a typical corporation, many things are done in ways that are unproductive, often because those ways used to be productive. Circumstances may have changed without accompanying changes in operations (or personalities.) Your company's management should welcome any suggestion of ways to increase the productivity of employees or machines. You probably know of some ways to increase productivity in your company. A suggestion to improve productivity is often an excellent way to receive recognition. That recognition should be considered bargaining chips to negotiate for more money or a different position.

## *Profitability*

A few of us hold the belief that corporations should not earn a profit. We think that profit, especially a large amount, indicates that the employees and/or customers are somehow being victimized.

In fact, a company cannot stay in business for long without earning a profit. Often, it must make more money each year to continue in business. If the company goes out of business, everyone there is out of work. Usually, anyone the corporation owes money to is also out of luck.

When a corporation is profitable, management can develop new product lines, which keeps the company competitive. Remaining competitive means continued sales. Profits also mean that people are employed and paid. The company can purchase needed equipment and supplies, which helps its suppliers remain in business. Shareholders receive dividends, and/or the value of their stock increases, making their investment secure. A profitable company pays taxes that support schools and other local functions. Companies also pay corporate taxes to the federal government, reducing the burden on individual taxpayers. In short, the profitability of corporate America is crucial to the success of our economy and our entire way of life.

If you have negative feelings about profit, try to evaluate why. The attitude that "everything should be fair" may be interfering with your judgment. You may see one company's profit as another's loss. You might know some managers who make decisions and knowingly or unknowingly hurt someone else in the name of profit. This does not make profit, or even high profit, evil. Profit is not intrinsically evil, it is simply profit. For a company to maintain employees, offer high-quality products and services to its customers, and continue to survive, profit is essential.

Don't assume that every existing firm is profitable. Some companies are in business for years before they introduce a product to the marketplace because it takes so long to develop their product. These companies are usually either supported by private investors or publicly owned. Sometimes they are owned entirely or in part by a larger, more profitable corporation that supports operations until they become profitable.

Other corporations have products to sell but do not sell enough to pay the bills. This might occur for several years in the beginning, or a company might have profitable years followed by losses. Many, many companies do not show a profit every quarter of every year. If you interview for a company that is not profitable, find out why. If the firm is publicly held, you can find financial information about it at the library or on the Internet before the interview. If not, you may have to talk with the interviewer about profit, or lack thereof. Don't automatically discard an opportunity because the company is not profitable, but find out what is going on before you jump at it.

Every employee should be interested in helping the company remain profitable. To be eligible for a highly paid job, you must see profitability as healthy and desirable, and you must be willing to work toward increased profitability. You must be able to think in terms of what you can contribute to profitability, not just the short-term welfare of you and those around you.

As a business person, try to see everything from the perspective of profit, and many things will begin to make sense. Some practices you now observe will make less sense, and you may be able to make a real difference.

## *Alternatives to the Word "Money"*

The term **investment** implies that we expect a purchase or expenditure ultimately to be worth more than we pay for it. We expect a return on our investment that is greater than the investment itself. For example, suppose a company spends $30,000 training you for a position as account manager. The company will consider that as an investment and expect you to generate more than $30,000 in profits as a result of your being hired and trained. Sometimes return is easy to determine. A certificate of deposit, for example, might pay 5% interest, or have a 5% return.

Sometimes the return on an investment is expressed in terms of time, such as an investment with a two-year return or a two-year payback. This means the investment is expected to break even in that amount of time and represent a profit after that. Let's say you buy a new piece of equipment for $3 million. You predict that the equipment will produce additional goods that will earn $1 million profit per year. Assuming that all the goods can be sold and your projections are accurate, the break-even point on the $3 million investment is three years. For decision-making purposes, the machine is expected to pay for itself in three years.

Get used to speaking in terms of investment, rather than spending. When you ask for a new computer, refer to it as an investment and your boss will be less likely to view it as just another expense. Begin to see your income and training as an investment that your company is making. You may be more likely to find ways to produce a measurable return.

Referring to something as **cost-effective** means the financial benefits outweigh the expenditure. Typically, we look for the most cost-effective way to operate, to maximize the return on our investment. For example, if you need to take a picture in Portugal, hiring a local photographer to do the job may be more cost-effective than flying the company photographer and crew there.

**Capital** usually refers to a large amount of money that is used or going to be used at one time. Examples of capital expenditures are purchasing a building, buying major equipment, and acquiring a new company. A company may have capital that is readily available or may need to borrow it. Typically, capital expenditures are treated differently from other expenses. Companies often have a separate budget for these items and designate only certain people to authorize capital expenses. Generally capital expenditures appear in a separate category in financial reports. As you make requests for purchases, you need to be aware of these differences. Sometimes funds are available for capital expenditures but not expense items, or vice versa.

Many times the terms *expense* and *cost* are used interchangeably. **Expense** has several connotations. Technically, it is a cost that is "used up" in an accounting period. Paper used in an office is an example of an expense. For tax purposes, we like to expense everything we can to decrease our tax liability.

In other instances, expense has a negative connotation as something that decreases profits.

## *Cash Flow*

**Cash flow** refers to the amount of cash available as a result of the timing of income and expenses. Managing cash flow can make or break a company. There are many companies with a sales volume plenty high enough to support their expenses, but they are financially crippled by the timing of cash flow.

Let's say you introduce a product that requires you to purchase materials from six different suppliers. It takes you three weeks to produce the product and another week to ship it to your wholesalers. If you are new to your suppliers or do not have good credit with them, you might have to pay them when you receive the raw materials, or even when you order them, which could be weeks before you receive them. Meanwhile you have to pay rent, utilities, wages, and other expenses associated with the manufacturing of your product. You then sell the product to wholesalers and incur sales costs. If your market is such that all your competitors operate on "net 30," meaning they have 30 days to pay after you send an invoice, that is probably the way you will have to do business. You have already paid dearly for this product even before you ship it out the door, and you now have to wait another 30 days to receive payment from your wholesalers.

This may seem like a simple example, but people who are not used to thinking in terms of cash flow might not understand the implications. Many large and small companies forfeit a lot of profit by not managing cash flow effectively.

Women often are privy to information concerning cash flow yet don't pay attention to it. We see it only as invoices and accounts payable or accounts receivable, but we should begin to recognize an opportunity. With a little research and calculations, you might be able to save money or earn more money for your company, simply by changing the way things are done.

I once worked for the branch of a large company, where we received checks from customers as down payment on our product. We did not cash those checks until after the product had been shipped, about six weeks later. Many times, we had tens of thousands of dollars in checks sitting in a drawer! This is an extreme example, but a real one. Perhaps you could suggest that your company start billing customers five days earlier and offer an incentive for prompt payment. Maybe you could propose moving money that must be held to an account where it could earn more interest.

Be aware of cash flow and its potential. You can gain a lot of points to use in bargaining for higher income if you can come up with a way to impact the bottom line.

**Liquidity** refers to how easily something can be turned into cash. Stocks and certificates of deposit, for example, can be converted into cash very easily, so they are considered very liquid, even if the company has to pay a penalty for early withdrawal. A company's plant and equipment are examples of assets not having much liquidity. If your creditors have you backed into a corner, it might take years to sell your manufacturing facility. A company is considered liquid when it has enough money to continue business for a period of time, even without sales revenue. It is always a difficult balance for a company to retain enough liquidity to pull through a possible dry spell while investing enough to grow and meet market demands. The consideration of liquidity is a part of business decisions. Note that when a company is **liquidated,** its various assets have been sold for cash to pay debts.

## *Income Statement Example*

The following is an example of a simple Income Statement, or Operating Statement, a financial report that public corporations provide to stockholders on a quarterly basis.

While this may be the only income statement you ever read, it is important to become familiar with each line item and what it means. These terms are used in business conversations all the time. You should understand them and feel comfortable using them in conversation yourself.

**Consolidated Statement of Income ABC Corp.**
Year ended September 30 ($ in thousands, except per share data)

| | **1996** | **1995** |
|---|---|---|
| Revenues | 146,044 | 93,106 |
| Cost of Sales | 85,034 | 51,322 |
| Gross margin | 61,010 | 41,784 |
| Operating expenses: | | |
| Research and development | 16,231 | 10,250 |
| Sales & Marketing | 24,128 | 19,270 |
| General and Administrative expenses | 5,883 | 4,747 |
| Total Operating expenses | 46,242 | 34,267 |
| Income (loss) from operations | 14,768 | 7,517 |
| Interest income | 1,159 | 67 |
| Interest and other expense, net | (1,233) | (807) |
| Income (loss) before income taxes | 14,694 | 6,777 |
| Provision for income taxes | 2,204 | 1,016 |
| Net income (loss) | 12,490 | 5,761 |
| Net income (loss) per share | .80 | .49 |
| Weighted average shares outstanding | 15,690 | 11,805 |

## *Income Statement Terms*

We will define the terms used in the Income Statement. Refer back to the sample income statement as you read these explanations.

**Revenue** refers to the dollars coming into the company from sales of products or services. This is a crucial number to any company. If a company cannot manage to sell enough stuff, eventually it will have to go out of business. The term almost always refers to a dollar amount before any expenses are deducted. Other sources of income, such as the interest a company earns or the sale of a company it owns (subsidiary,) are not usually referred to as revenue, or they are shown separately from sales revenue. This is because sales revenue needs to be measured on its own, not distorted by other income. Sometimes revenue is shown separately for individual products or product lines. Revenue received is compared to corporate revenue goals and to previous financial periods, as in our example. The term **sales**, or sometimes **net sales**, may be used interchangeably with the word *revenue*.

**Costs** are deducted from this revenue figure. An income statement includes many different kinds of costs, but the cost of sales is an important one. In our income statement example, the **cost of sales** would include all the raw materials that went into the making of a product and all wages paid to produce it. In our example, the cost of sales includes only what it cost to make it, not what it cost to sell it. It seems confusing, since the word sales is part of the term, but it refers to the cost of the product which was sold. These are also referred to as **direct costs**, since these costs would not be incurred if the product were not being manufactured. Somehow, we need to determine how much it cost us to produce our products or a specific product line. Only then can we begin to determine if it is profitable.

At this point, let's consider cost in general. Cost is usually an extremely complex concept. There are certified public accountants who specialize in cost accounting. You will appear very naive if you assume that the cost a company incurs for its product or service is cut-and-dried.

Consider this example: You have just spent $3 million to develop a new type of contact lens. You need a $500,000 machine to manufacture it, and the materials to make it cost $0.04 per pair from the plastics manufacturer. What is your cost for these lenses? What price should you charge? Legally there may be different ways to determine cost. Two companies with the same sales and expenses can make and show varying amounts of profit on specific products or product lines, depending on how they cost their goods or services on paper.

Determining costs may be easier for retailers than for manufacturers, since retailers are charged a certain amount for the merchandise they receive from wholesalers and distributors. If you are a retailer, however, how much does it cost you to carry this item in inventory? How much did you pay for the money (interest) to buy from the wholesaler? What other items are you not buying because you have your money tied up in this merchandise?

How does cost compare to **price**? Consider our contact lens example. What do we charge for this product, for which we have invested over $3.5 million? The answer: Price is determined by the market in which we operate. We will charge what we believe people are willing to pay for these lenses, no matter what they've cost us. The price of competitive or similar products can help us set our price. If we can't keep our costs within our price and make a profit, we will have to go out of business or find something else to sell. Raising our price because our costs increased only works if our competitors do the same.

Knowing these two things, that cost is complex and price is determined by the market, will give you an advantage over many men and women with whom you compete for jobs. Never use the words *price* and *cost* interchangeably in conversation. Others may make that mistake, but you should not.

Returning to our income statement example, **gross margin**, or **gross profit**, refers to the company's sales revenue after subtracting the direct cost of making the product. We need to measure this to see how successful our product or service is at any particular time. It is called *gross*, in the sense of an all-inclusive total, because other expenses have yet to be subtracted from it.

The next several items on the income statement example are **operating expenses**, which will be subtracted from the gross profit figure.

**Research and development** is a major operating expense in some industries. Companies in the software industry, for example, will spend a substantial portion of revenue on research and development of new products. While programmers' salaries are listed as costs, you can be sure the programmers themselves are considered line personnel.

**Sales and marketing** expenses refer to the advertising, sales brochures, salespeople's income, and expenses directly incurred in selling the product. Our income statement example is for an entire company, but companies also consider sales and marketing expenses separately for individual products or product lines.

**General and administrative costs** are lumped together in our example. This category includes administrative and support services, equipment such as computers and copiers, supplies, and expenses such as rent and electricity. These items might be separated in some income statements, and they might be separated for different product lines. The salaries here are paid to staff people. Some or all of these costs are considered **fixed costs**, because the costs are incurred, even if nothing at all is sold. The costs don't change with various sales volumes. Sometimes these costs are allocated evenly or equitably between departments. Sometimes one division will reflect more of these costs on its records than another, to make the second division look more profitable. How costs are allocated is often a source of disagreement among managers, who are accountable for their own bottom line. Another word for these types of expenses is **overhead.** The term overhead generally has a negative connotation, since it decreases the company's bottom line, rather than adding to it. Your current position may be considered overhead. Every corporation has some overhead, and management constantly seeks ways to reduce it.

All these operating expenses are added together and shown as **total operating expenses**.

That figure is then subtracted from the gross profit to come up with **total operating income (or loss.)** If the figure is below zero, it is put in parentheses, or the letter *d* (for deficit) appears just before the figure. This operating income is separated from other income, because it reflects the sales of the company and how well those sales supported the expenses of the company. For example, if your company sold a subsidiary (a company it owns,) there might be plenty of money to support expenses and show a profit, but it would be a one-time source of income. The selling of products and services must continue in order for a company to survive, and sales-related revenue and expenses must be measured separately.

**Interest income,** or interest earned on cash, could be huge, if the company holds a lot of cash, or a much smaller figure. Unless you are in charge of investing the cash, you probably won't need to know or be concerned about it. As with other figures not directly related to sales, interest income is broken out separately from revenue so it doesn't distort sales figures.

Interest paid on loans, along with other miscellaneous expenses, is listed as **interest and other expense, net**. This is subtracted from the two previous income line items to give us **income (or loss) before income taxes**. In this case, the terms *profit* and *income* are used interchangeably. It is important for individuals to know what they make before taxes, and it is equally important for a corporation to know what it makes.

The next line item shows the company's **provision for income taxes**., or what the corporation is obligated to pay the IRS for the accounting period.

That figure is subtracted from *income (or loss) before income taxes* to determine the bottom line: the company's **net income or (loss.)** This is the **profit** for the corporation for the specified time period.

It is from this report, the income statement, that the phrase **bottom line** originates. Expenses are deducted from income sources, and the result is at the bottom of the page. You will hear the phrase *bottom line* a lot, and it has come to mean the end result of just about anything. When we are *bottom-line oriented*, we are looking to maximize profit. We want to increase sales and control costs.

Since the company in our example is a publicly held corporation, the profit is divided by the number of shares at the time to come up with a **net income per share**. Shareholders are more concerned than employees with this figure, unless they are the same people.

The last line item on the income statement, **weighted average number of shares outstanding**, refers to the number of shares available to trade at any given time. In our example, ABC Corporation apparently added 4 million shares during 1996. This dilutes the value of everyone's holdings, but allows the corporation to offer stock options to employees or raise additional cash by selling shares to the public. The decision to change the number of shares outstanding must be voted on and approved by shareholders.

A few other terms should be discussed here. **Profit margin** refers to the profit as a percentage of revenue. If you sell a contract for $500,000 that produces $50,000 in profit after all expenses are deducted, your profit margin is 10% (profit divided by sales.) Not surprisingly, some companies pay attention to gross profit margin, net profit margin before taxes, and net profit margin after taxes. Some divisions have specific profit margins to meet each year. When you hear someone speak of margin or margins, think of profit margin. Whether it is gross, net before taxes, after-tax, or some other configuration, you will need to find out.

I have seen highly intelligent people sacrifice enormous profits to maintain profit margin. I once knew a service manager whose performance was measured on profit margin. He would refuse to do a job with a $100,000 profit if the margin was only 10%, but would welcome a $10,000 job with a profit margin of 25%. This is an example of how short-sighted we can be when it comes to the measurement of our jobs. This manager's department made less money than it could have, but he wanted it that way. He was measured not on the dollar amount of profits to the company, but on profit margin. If you find ourself in a similar position, you should approach executives about changing the standard of measurement.

Notice in our example that the year ends September 30. The **fiscal year** is a full business year. Some corporations choose to begin their fiscal year on a day other than January 1. The year always begins on the first day of a month. A fiscal year may run from July 1 to June 30, or from October 1 to September 30, or whatever period chosen. When referring to the fiscal year, use the calendar year in which it ends. For example, the fiscal year that runs from July 1, 1997, to June 30, 1998, is called *fiscal 1998*.

The fiscal year is divided into four **fiscal quarters** of three months each, beginning the first day of the fiscal year. For example, if the fiscal year is July 1 to June 30, the first quarter would run from July 1 to September 30, the second from October 1 to December 31, and so on. Occasionally, a corporation will use a fiscal year other than the calendar year for financial reporting, but use the calendar year for certain budgets. If you are involved in budgeting or forecasting, it is imperative to know the time frame. If your request for new equipment is denied because of budget restraints, you need to know when the new budget kicks in.

Almost every business is seasonal to some extent; rarely do companies receive revenues and profits in a nice smooth influx over time. For this reason, management will compare results from the current fiscal quarter to those from the same fiscal quarter one year ago. For example, a financial report for the second quarter of this year would compare sales and profit figures to those of the second quarter of last year, and perhaps the year before. If you compare results of this quarter to those of last quarter only, you might make false assumptions about the company's success.

## *Balance Sheet Example*

The following is an example of a **balance sheet**. This report is available to shareholders on a quarterly and annual basis. It describes the value of a company at any given point in time, as well as is possible. Some of these terms may be used in conversations you have with your colleagues.

**Consolidated Balance Sheet of ABC Corporation**
(in thousands)

| | **1996** | **1995** |
|---|---|---|
| ASSETS | | |
| Current assets: | | |
| Cash and cash equivalents | 12,237 | 863 |
| Accounts receivable, net for doubtful accounts | 41,811 | 22,183 |
| Inventories | 37,391 | 16,248 |
| Total current assets | 91,439 | 39,294 |
| Property, plant, and equipment less depreciation | 7,703 | 5,683 |
| Total assets | 99,142 | 44,977 |
| LIABILITIES AND SHAREHOLDERS EQUITY | | |
| Current liabilities: | | |
| Accounts payable | 8,912 | 15,370 |
| Accrued expenses | 3,298 | 1,719 |
| Income tax payable | 550 | 3,535 |
| Total current liabilities | 12,760 | 20,624 |
| Long term-term obligations | 10,195 | 23,563 |
| Stockholder's equity | 76,187 | 790 |

## *Balance Sheet Terms*

In a financial context the term **current** means within the present accounting period. **Current assets** are **cash** or those things which are expected to be turned into cash in this accounting period. The accounting period could be one month, one quarter, or, as in our example, one year.

The **current accounts receivable** item refers to monies that are owed to the corporation and expected to be paid in this accounting period. Any bills (invoices) that have been sent to customers but not yet collected would be included in this line item. As noted in the example, doubtful accounts are deducted from these. The longer someone goes without paying you, the more doubtful the account becomes. Without deducting these doubtful accounts, the financial strength of your business might be misrepresented.

**Inventory** represents a lot of physical items, although it is given as a monetary value on the balance sheet. There are several different kinds of inventory, such as raw materials (things you buy from suppliers, before you use them to make your products,) goods in process (partly completed,) finished goods, and other indirect supplies. Not all companies have all kinds of inventory. Inventory is often a major expense and is sometimes difficult to manage. There are various legal ways to cost inventory, and different inventory costing techniques can dramatically change a company's bottom line. With better technology, many corporations are using what is referred to as *just-in-time inventory*. Materials and parts are ordered just before they are needed for manufacturing, and arrive just as they are needed. This has saved millions of dollars of inventory costs.

You may have a lot of information about inventory and how well or poorly it is managed. It may be time to impact the bottom line with your suggestions.

We add the current assets together to come up with the **total current assets** figure, and then move on to noncurrent, or long-term, assets.

A corporation's **property, plant, and equipment** are considered assets, although they are not current assets since they are not easily converted to cash. The same long-term asset may be listed on the balance sheet with a different value each year because it has been depreciated, in the same way that your car is worth less each year you own it.

Financial reports must reflect what took place during a specified time frame. Otherwise, they wouldn't mean much. Some items, such as a building or a copy machine, last awhile. An attempt is made to reflect what portion of an item was "used up" during the accounting period in question (month, quarter, year.) A certain amount is allocated, regardless of what money (if any) was actually spent on the asset during the time frame. This used-up value is deducted from last accounting period's value to determine the value of the asset. There are three terms that describe the allocation: depreciation, amortization, and depletion.

Of the three terms, you probably see the term **depreciation** most often. This one is used in our example. This term applies to physical objects. Buildings, computers, and anything else expected to last beyond a year or so are usually depreciated. The IRS dictates the length of time over which we can depreciate an item, based on an estimated life for items in the same category. The length of time is shorter for items like computers that quickly become obsolete, than for items such as buildings that are expected to be used for a longer time. Legally, some items must be depreciated in a certain way. For other things, a company has a choice of ways to depreciate the item. The choice can affect the reported bottom line. These are decisions for the accountant.

The allocation is called **amortization** when it refers to an intangible item. If you hold a patent on a product, for example, you will "use up" a part of this patent during each quarter and each year until it expires. The value of the patent is determined and then amortized over the life of the patent. For each accounting period, a portion (not necessarily equal portion) of this value shows up as an amortization allowance. You are gradually using up something of value. This does not actually cost the company money, but it appears as an expense. It is a deduction from revenues, therefore decreases the company's tax liability.

A **depletion** allowance is used for natural resources that a corporation owns. For example, it may be estimated that a certain oil well will produce oil for 20 years, and this asset (the well) will be depleted over that time. If you are still pumping oil from the well after 20 years, you will have no depletion allowance to deduct from your revenues. If the well is still producing enough, you probably will not shut it down, but you will no longer have a depletion allowance to offset the revenue. You will pay taxes accordingly.

Unless you are an accountant, you will not need to determine these allocations. You may never hear of them again, but you might. Because they represent deductions from revenues and may be far different from actual cash expenditures, they have an impact on the cash flow of your company. For instance, if you pay $700,000 cash in 1999 for a new robotic system, that capital will not be available for other purposes. According to the income statement, however, you will have an expense that is far less than $700,000. It might be important for you to know where these figures came from.

Returning to the balance sheet example, we add all our assets, both current and long-term, together and compare them to our **liabilities**.

Liabilities are those items that we have not spent money on yet, but we know we will. **Current liabilities** are those obligations payable within the accounting period in question. They must be paid soon. As our year ends, we have some bills we have not paid. These are **accounts payable**, or A/P.

In our example, ABC Corporation has an obligation to pay some employees for time and benefits, so these are listed under **accrued expenses**. In other words, some people have put in time that has not been paid for. Even if they have already quit, the expense has been incurred, and they will have to be paid. In addition, there is income tax owed, perhaps for the fourth quarter, which has yet to be paid. There is a difference in timing between when taxes are due and when the accounting period ends. It is advantageous to hold onto our money as long as possible and pay things only as they are due, but we must list those obligations we have.

We add these together to get **total current liabilities**.

The next line item in the example shows our **long-term obligations**, which are the dollars we have committed to pay over a long-term contract, such as the lease on a building or equipment. We haven't paid this money yet, but to leave it off the balance sheet would misrepresent the financial strength of the company. That money is not available to be used for anything else.

Our liabilities are added together, and the difference between the assets and liabilities is the **stockholder's equity**. This is an oversimplification, but this is one way to measure the value of the corporation at a given time.

You may not be reading financial reports on a regular basis, but you may hear and use these terms in a business setting. Become familiar with the terms used in your company and your industry. Your intelligent use of financial terms will help others take you more seriously and see you for potential beyond your current position.

*"If you have been out of college for years and are thinking of going back to school, should you? You certainly should not-not unless you know exactly what you are doing and why."*[1]

CHAPTER 6

# Off to College?

So, you want to make a career change. The first thing you should do is enter college, right? Women are entering colleges and technical schools in droves. Women who are currently employed, as well as those reentering the job market, are taking courses and studying, confident that this education is their eventual ticket to success.

As an adult, earning a degree requires making enormous sacrifices to your financial, social, and emotional well-being. Sometimes, additional training or education is just what we need. Other times, however, our reasons for going back to school are not valid. Learn to examine your reasons for returning to school, just as you examine your reasons for acting and reacting in other ways. You might find that your reasons are a result of female conditioning, rather than logical, appropriate decisions.

1. Harragan, Betty Lehan. (1977). *Games Mother Never Taught You: Corporate Gamesmanship for Women* (p. 216). New York: Warner Books.

Maybe you are interested in returning to college for one of these reasons:

- You believe a certain education will bring you opportunities that you don't have now.
- You think a degree will help you gain a level of confidence or competence that you don't have currently.
- You don't know what you want to do, and you want to go to college to find out.
- Someone recommended that you go to college.
- You want to be in college.

Let's take a look at what's behind each of these reasons.

## *A Degree Means Opportunity?*

As an adult who wants to change the direction of your career and earn more for your efforts, this may seem like a logical first step. It may even be true. There are American corporations with policies against having non-degreed personnel in many positions. In some cases, any old degree will do. However, there are many other corporations which do not have those policies. It might be easier to change companies than to get a degree. Remember, most positions in business are filled by people with a variety of educational backgrounds.

Too many of us earn a degree which doesn't lead to a career, and then take a job which never needed the degree. Currently, there are hundreds of thousands of women studying to be teachers who will never work in that field. This is not because they lack the desire, but because there are so few opportunities. People who probably consider themselves risk-adverse are investing enormous amounts to prepare for something they have a very slim chance of attaining. An elementary principal told me recently she had 1,000 applications for two positions. Most of these women will do something else for a living. They will accept lower pay than they should because they believe they do not have the necessary training for a "professional" business position.

As we read the statistics, we know that the more education men complete, the more money they are likely to make. On the average, their income goes up with education. Men with degrees in liberal arts or education fill male-dominated jobs in corporate America. Women with these same degrees fill female jobs. We are labeled as unqualified, we figure it must be our degree. We need to prove how qualified we are. This is usually easier than earning another degree.

Two years of training in computer programming could mean *much* more to your paycheck than a bachelor's degree in liberal arts. If you ask people what training meant the most to their career, it is often not college, but the training provided by their current or previous employers, or a smattering of courses taken at various places.

If you are going to college, make sure you earn a degree which will, in fact, enhance your career. Don't study things you think are fun and then expect a degree to help you make a living.

The following positions were recently cited as the most frequently advertised positions with salaries in the upper-middle- to high-income range: programmers, systems analysts, data processing specialists, computer graphics designers, microprocessing technicians, telecommunications specialists, software specialists, electronic engineers, civil engineers, computer hardware engineers, product design engineers, systems engineers, marketing managers, district regional managers, marketing analysts, marketing research specialists, internal auditors, controllers, corporate tax accountants, financial analysts, investment professionals, loan officers, new business development analysts, bank managers, economic analysts, international banking officers, technical writers, health care specialists, technical support managers, fiber optics scientists, petroleum geologists, and ceramic technicians.

The requirements for these positions vary. Some require a specific college degree, while others require certain work experience or technical training. Many of these jobs have no specific educational requirements. None of these positions specifically requires a degree in liberal arts or education.

Especially if you do not have a degree now, don't earn one unless it is in a specific field which in fact holds opportunities. If you are going to take the time, effort, and money to go back to college, make sure it will pay off! Higher education is a top priority for so many women, and yet the great majority of us remain in low-paying careers. What's going on?

The world of business is filled with individuals with every level of education, working side by side. People with high school diplomas often fill the same positions as people with MBAs. They may have similar work experience, or they may have made similar impressions on the people who hire and promote. People with a high school education are promoted over people with more education all the time, for lots of reasons. In a Gallup poll, chief executives from various-sized companies were asked, "What does it take to get ahead?" Education was ranked eighth out of eight on their list of answers. The top two reasons in every case were integrity and the ability to get along with others. If you are over 25, your work experience and abilities will weigh much more heavily on your resume than your education. Perhaps you believe you have no experience. You probably need to learn to present your background in a more favorable way.

The fields of education and health care are filled with women, and many of us move into business from these two fields. Educational requirements for education and health care positions are usually clear-cut. In most cases, each job requires a very specific educational background. You can't become a principal, teacher, occupational therapist, registered nurse, or surgeon without the right degree. I believe one reason that women are so likely to go back to school is that we assume specific educational requirements exist in the business world as well. The fact is, when we leave health care or education to pursue a career in business, the educational requirements often become much more vague.

## *A Degree Means Confidence and Competence*

Getting a degree seems like a simple, if not easy, solution. The lack of an education is one of those concrete, well-defined excuses for not being where we want to be. It's easier to use this excuse than to evaluate our self-image or change our approach. We like to think there is a sure-fire way to get where we want to go, a straight path that no one will question. Life in the business world is not like that.

Maybe you anticipate that more education will give you the confidence and competence you lack. Surely all that time in the classroom must teach you something. You may be convinced that what you will learn is exactly what you don't know now, but need to know. The knowledge you need to perform the job is lurking somewhere on campus.

Carefully examine your lack of confidence in a specific field or job. Even if you spend the next four years of your life in a classroom, you can be sure of this: the first question in your first job interview out of school will be about your work experience. The time, effort, and money needed to complete more formal education can often be spent more efficiently elsewhere.

You may feel insecure about not having much education. When groups of people over 30 years old work together, they seldom discuss formal education. They may work side by side for years without knowing or caring who has a degree or in what or from where. Not surprisingly, the people without a college degree often make it more of an issue than those who have one. Successful people have told me of their fears of being "found out" as they work with college-educated people. Meanwhile, the people they worry about recognize their abilities to perform the job.

Don't assume the people around you know or care whether you have graduated from college. If they know that you haven't, they may admire you all the more for being so successful without a degree. Don't get a college education just because you think it will make you feel better. The sacrifices may not be worth it. If it does not help your chances for advancement, you certainly won't feel better. Don't allow a lack of education to pull your confidence level down. Don't be the one who makes your lack of education an issue.

Before you sacrifice your life savings and your social life for the coveted degree, direct some of that time, energy, and money toward developing your career with the education you now have. Invest in some corporate clothes. Spend some time and energy on your self-image, your self-confidence, and your attitude. Find out what other people do for a living. Go after some new jobs, lots of them, and see what happens.

There are many alternatives to returning to college full-time. If you need specific skills or knowledge, take a course or two. Ask your employer to pay the tuition. Try taking a correspondence course or attending a seminar. Join a professional organization.

## *College Will Help Me Define My Goals*

Women are often led to college by well-meaning people who convince us we are confused. We are too seldom in positions that expose us to the total workings of a corporation. We often decide to make choices later than the men around us, because we have spent time waiting for others to tell us what to do. We don't even know what there is to choose from when we get around to choosing. When we try to gain some direction, we are asked all kinds of questions that do not apply directly to anyone's career goals. When we come up empty-handed, college seems to be the only place to figure it out. If only we had a higher education, or more education, or a different degree, we would be able to clarify what we want out of life.

The ivory tower is a far cry from the business world. Many people there have never worked outside a university, and their experience in business may be more limited than yours. Course material will teach you something about the opportunities that exist, but not nearly as efficiently as you can learn on your own. Do some investigative work on where the jobs are. If you don't want to, do it anyway. Being in a male job track is about taking initiative, while being in a female job track is about taking orders. The entire process may take a few months, but remember that completing formal education can take years.

## *They Told Me To*

Maybe you are considering college because someone recommended that you do so. Who made this recommendation? Perhaps it was someone you admire or someone who does the job you would like to do. Perhaps it was your boss. Perhaps it was your husband or a parent. When we already feel insecure, halfway convinced that we need more education, an offhand comment from almost anyone can cause us to run to the nearest college to enroll.

Whatever the source, carefully examine your need to attend college before enrolling. Maybe a woman who told you to go to college has a degree that she earned between the ages of 18 and 22, when she had no family and no significant financial commitments. Perhaps a degree helped her to get where she is, but that does not mean it is necessary for you at this point in your life.

Perhaps you have been told you were turned down from a job you applied for because you did not have the right formal education. This may have been just a handy excuse to give you. Maybe they wanted a man instead, or maybe you interviewed poorly and did not impress the interviewer. It's possible the person they hired had no more education than you have. It is easy to let others convince us that a degree will put us on the path to success. Meanwhile, we are losing out on opportunities in the job path of our choice, because our time and attention is on our studies.

It may seem that going to school buys you some time. As long as you are in school, you are working toward your goal, without having to take the plunge and start your new career just yet. Examine this motive. If you want a male career path, you need to get used to acting before you are completely sure of yourself, taking risks, and assuming responsibility for the results. Going to college to bide your time until you are completely ready sounds just like a woman.

Maybe there is a specific job you really want, but the employer wants you to have a certain education for it. If that is the only thing standing between you and that job, why not offer to go to school while you are on the job, with the employer paying tuition? Obviously, you can learn more and your education will be more fruitful if you can apply the theory as you learn it. If this is impossible, ask what position the company can offer you while you attend school and the employer pays your tuition. Ask how soon can you move into the position you want. Don't go back to college just because somebody somewhere said you needed to get some sort of degree for some job you thought you wanted.

## *I Like School*

Sometimes we go back to school because we want to be there. College or graduate school is a safe haven, where success is easily defined, as in grades. There, we do not have to develop strategies to get ahead in an environment of subjective evaluations and unspoken rules, as in the business world. Our intellects might be challenged, but we don't have to put our knowledge to the test with real-life situations. We have stimulating, demanding work, but it comes to a complete conclusion every semester. Typically, we compete only with ourselves. Our projects are not held up by another's inefficient or incomplete efforts. College is as fair as almost any place we can find. If you want to go to school for its own sake, do it. Work hard and enjoy it, but don't fool yourself into believing you have another motive.

## *Just Examine Your Reasons*

Certainly, there is nothing inherently wrong with education, or earning a degree. If you are just out of high school and have the opportunity to go to college, go ahead and learn as much as you can. You will not be sorry. Study a specific curriculum that leads to a career, one with opportunities for promotion and the potential for you to earn enough to support yourself.

If you do not have a high school diploma, I strongly suggest you earn it or get the equivalent. No one can fault you for dropping out of high school years ago, when you had the problems and judgement of most teen-agers. But a high school diploma is perceived by most of the business world as a basic requirement, and it's relatively easy to obtain. You can get information on studying for and taking the GED exam from your local public school district.

College education is great, but something else might be better for you right now. Carefully examine your situation before enrolling.

***"Powerful men also plan for contingencies. If strategy one doesn't work, what next? They select, beforehand, strategy two and three. Our experience with women shows their reluctance to play the game is based upon their having only one strategy. When it fails, they are left high and dry with their private or public humiliation."[1]***

CHAPTER 7

# Negotiate With the Best

When it comes to negotiating, we often find ourselves at a disadvantage as women. First, we lack finesse in this area, having little experience with negotiating. Second, we are unaware that negotiations are even taking place. The results of these handicaps are enormous. Not only are we less likely to gain what we need in a situation, others see us as unable to perform the job – apparently unqualified.

For years authors on the topic have told us that women are poor negotiators. If it is true for you, it is standing in the way of your success.

We take what is said to us as gospel truth, when, in fact, it may simply be a negotiating tactic. When we have to plead our

1. Melia & Lyttle. (1986). *Why Jenny Can't Lead* (p. 150). Grand Junction, CO: Operational Politics.

case, we either give in or stamp our feet and stand our ground. The concepts of negotiation, give-and-take, and trade-off all represent foreign territory to us.

In fact, negotiating is an intrinsic part of American business. We need the skill to perform many results-oriented jobs. Inherent in every corporation are conflicting agendas and goals, coupled with limited resources. Negotiating is necessary to a businesswoman's survival.

This chapter presents skills and tactics to use in negotiating. The more easily you can recognize the negotiations going on around you, the sooner you will be prepared to participate.

To demonstrate, I have created two scenarios. The first assumes that you are negotiating for a raise. The second has you requesting that management create a position that you have designed. For the sake of discussion, we'll assume your boss is a woman.

No matter what the negotiating circumstances, consider all the skills and strategies discussed. For the newcomer – a category that includes most of us – this information may seem overwhelming. This chapter is designed not to overpower you, but to increase your awareness of what is going on around you and prepare you to participate. Awareness and preparation can be your allies.

## *An Increase in Salary*

If you have never asked for a raise, you are not alone. Women everywhere are working hard, expecting that our efforts will be recognized on their own merits. We accept whatever is offered. Many of us have learned to live within the confines of our salaries gracefully, if not comfortably. We try to value our work in other than monetary terms, convincing ourselves that more pay might cause us to become materialistic. Meanwhile, some men and women around us have learned the importance of valuing their skills highly, requesting raises, and negotiating for them. The gap between our income and theirs widens.

You may believe it is unnecessary or undesirable to negotiate for more income. You may view requesting a raise as "unfeminine" or think that someone else (your boss) will take care of you. To ask for a raise would be to question the judgment of those who have determined your income. Because you do not perform your job perfectly, 100% of the time, you may believe you cannot justify a raise.

Many of us also have to overcome the feeling that we don't deserve what we ask for. Lack of entitlement may be keeping you from asking for a higher income. You must learn to do it anyway. This is the way the game is played. You did not write the rules. Learn the rules, and learn to play. You are a valued member of the team. If you are not valued, you should find out as soon as possible.

We must see getting a raise as our responsibility, not someone else's problem. In business, money is considered a motivator of workers. No corporation wants to pay more than necessary, but managers know they must pay good people to keep them.

So, how do you begin?

The first step in asking for a raise is to make an appointment to do so. Tell your boss you have something you need to discuss and allocate some time. Without an appointment, you may not have your manager's full attention. If you simply walk into her office and make it a casual conversation, your boss is likely to see it as unimportant.

Timing is everything. You know your boss best. Schedule the appointment to your best advantage. If you have recently accomplished something worthy of recognition, strike while the iron is hot.

Don't assume that your coworkers will be on your side when it comes to salary negotiations. If they find out you asked for a raise, they may be jealous because they do not have the nerve to do so. You can be sure they will be right behind you with the argument, "You gave Susan a raise, now I want one." When you negotiate for more money, your income is the only one at stake. Maybe the boss can justify an additional $3,000 for you, but not for each and every one in the department. You will lose credibility if you discuss this with your coworkers, and credibility is crucial in all future negotiations. Keep it to yourself.

## *Prepare and Rehearse*

Each of us improves with practice, no matter what the skill. Women are often guilty of assuming that other people were somehow born with the business skills they have. We can't envision our male colleagues practicing at home with their wives. We also don't like to take the time to practice.

If you are preparing to negotiate for a raise, practice. The payoff can be enormous. The results can affect not only your immediate income, but all future income with this company. Practice either in front of a mirror or with a friend, but do some preparation. Your confidence will improve, and that will allow you to remain calm and listen clearly when the time comes.

You may be afraid that what you say will sound memorized, but it is much more likely that you will sound natural. Having practiced your phrasing, it will flow out of your mouth, even in a tense situation. Without rehearsal, you may find yourself groping for words when you most need fluency.

One of the most persuasive people I know often begins her sentences with the word "clearly." This word indicates that the point she is about to make is obvious to all. To question her would be questioning the obvious, and no one wants to appear stupid. Phrases such as "I'm sure you understand" can have much the same impact. Try interjecting some of these kinds of words and phrases into your speech. You will appear more confident, and your listeners will be more likely to accept what you have to say. You may also be replacing some destructive phrases such as "you know." Just be careful not to overuse a word or phrase.

## *Silence is Golden*

Rehearse what you want to say, and practice your response to what you anticipate will be said to you. Finally, practice remaining silent. Maintaining silence can be very difficult when you are trying to convince someone, make a good impression, and win approval. However, it is very important.

Accept silence as a part of serious negotiating. Welcome it as a sign that things are going well. Resist the urge to jump in and fill the gap, especially if you were the last one to speak. Silence both before and after you speak can add impact that no amount of words could accomplish. Many people believe that the first one who talks after a silence, loses.

When the hour has arrived, stand tall, take three slow and deep breaths, and enter your boss's office. You have everything to gain and almost nothing to lose. You are a strong, capable woman. What you ask is not unreasonable.

## *Emphasize Accomplishments*

Emphasize your accomplishments.Your personal need for a raise is not the issue. Discard the long-held belief that if you work hard, your efforts will be rewarded. Corporations need to make a profit. Resources should be allocated toward that end. The more you contribute to the profits of the corporation, the more you deserve to be paid. Although we can find many exceptions, that is still the premise on which business operates. It's hard for most women to trace their accomplishments to profits.

Build your case on your contributions to the company and to the team. As you prepare, quantify your results as much as possible. Attach numbers to everything and anything you can think of. "My suggestion for pre-filing has saved 10 hours per week." Even if you cannot take credit for everything, you can say, "My contributions helped this department enjoy a 20% increase in efficiency this year." Remember to talk in terms of results, not effort. The fact that you work long hours does not necessarily mean that you accomplish more. Think of yourself as part of a team, and try not to compare yourself to others. Making a statement like, "My work is much more accurate than Susan's," will usually put you in a bad light.

Line jobs can be traced to profit more readily than staff positions, and so they tend to pay more across the board. As discussed, women tend to gravitate toward staff positions, often ignorant of this discrepancy in income. I believe women would demand more if they could more easily measure the impact of their efforts. Male or female, those who can relate our efforts directly to the bottom line can demand more for our time and get it. Keep this in mind as you examine new career possibilities.

In the meantime, you may be having trouble showing just how you have brought in more revenue or saved more dollars. Those around you (including your boss) may have the same problem measuring their own success in terms of profitability. If you can't relate your job directly to the company's profits, don't give up. Emphasize your contributions to the group effort. Without you, reports would not be compiled on time, or forecasts could not be presented. Call attention to everything that stands out about your work. This is not the time to be humble. Do not expect your work to speak for itself. Your boss has a thousand things to do besides monitor the results of your efforts. That is your job, and so is passing along the information.

Avoid the temptation to ask for a raise based on your needs. It may be true that your rent has been raised or your child care costs have increased, but these are not reasons for the company to pay you more. It is no one's business how you intend to spend the additional money. People in this country are not paid according to their needs. Concentrate on why you deserve a raise. You will be taken more seriously, and your argument will not be diluted in the eyes of the employer.

Don't use the argument that you deserve a raise because you have not received one in two years. Focus on the results of your performance. Preparation can help. List all the ways in which you have contributed, so that you can add to your case as the negotiations continue.

If you have not had a performance review in a while, ask for one. This can help pave the way for asking for a raise. After all, your request for more income is based on the results of your performance, so the two go hand in hand. While many of us dread performance reviews, they are crucial to know where we stand and how we might improve. This is an excellent chance to find out what your boss might not otherwise tell you.

As you point out your accomplishments, be prepared for criticism of your work. None of us does our job perfectly, and some of us put our best efforts in the wrong direction entirely.

Criticism can be the most valuable information you gain. Your reaction to criticism will greatly affect the outcome of negotiations. Ask for specific examples, so that it becomes clear to both you and your manager where you need to improve. This may not be easy for your boss, so don't become defensive even if you disagree. Take time later to digest it all. Accept criticism as an opportunity to improve, even if you believe it is intended otherwise. Don't forget that your objective is to receive more money on payday. Relax, use the skills you have practiced, and listen to what is said.

## *Determine the Other Person's Needs*

Rehearsal includes not only preparing your argument, but also trying to anticipate the opposition's argument. If women are truly more other-oriented, we should find this easier than most men. Determine your boss's position and anticipate the corresponding arguments. Prepare for the arguments you might receive. The more you can anticipate objections, the more calmly you can answer them as they come up. You will also be more capable of smoothly handling unexpected objections. Don't just prepare a speech of the points you want to make. Prepare to uncover your manager's arguments and address them one by one.

Chastain names the three most common objections from managers when employees ask for a raise:

1. It's not in the budget.
2. Other employees aren't making that much.
3. It's a lot more than you've been making.

Let's take a look at how you might answer these objections.

## *Not in the Budget*

Women too often see the budget as some kind of divine mandate, partly because we are so far-removed from the budget-making process. We don't know how the budget is determined, what people are involved in its negotiation, or what part they play. We often don't even know when one budget cycle ends and another begins. We have no idea how much money is in the budget overall or how specific dollars are allocated for individual items, such as our salaries. We have no idea how flexible the budget is, how often it is reviewed, or what happens when budget amounts are exceeded. In spite of these unknowns, we stubbornly view the amount budgeted for our salaries as cast in stone. The word *budget*, often used in negotiating, can cause us to retreat instantly from our demands.

So how do you answer this objection? You will almost assuredly hear it, since the budget is probably an important part of your boss's day. From her perspective, citing budget restrictions is a good argument or at least puts her in a good bargaining position. To some degree the budget is out of her hands. She does not have to assume responsibility for your lousy salary or the inability to give you a raise. There's no need even to come up with reasons why your performance does not warrant a raise. "A raise is impossible at this time because the budget does not allow it. I'm sure you understand." Don't panic. This may simply be a negotiating tactic. Start to find out more by asking questions.

## *Ask Questions*

Remember that what is volunteered to you may not be completely true, it may be a negotiating strategy. This is one of the most important lessons to learn. Some of us tend to be completely honest and expect others to do the same. We see any deviation from the truth as lying. In fact, negotiating may be taking place, and we are expected to participate. Learn to ask questions to determine your boss's position.

Ask if a specific amount is allocated to salaries, or a range of dollars. Ask if monies can be shifted from one area to another. If another employee has recently left your department, the salary and benefits allocated for that person should be available. If your department has cut costs in some other way, or could cut costs, inquire if some of that savings could be shifted to your salary. Ask how flexible the budget is. What happens when additional funds are needed? What process does your boss follow to increase the budget for your department? When is the budget reviewed? When is it formalized? If nothing else works, ask whether your request can become a part of the next budget request process.

This approach may seem bold to you. You may be told that the budget is none of your business, or, worse yet, not to worry your pretty little head about it. The truth is, the budget is your business. You are expected to live within your salary. You need to know how it is determined and how much flexibility exists. You may make your boss uncomfortable with this line of questioning, but that is part of the process. Don't turn into a bully, but don't back down just because your boss squirms. Women have been known to sacrifice everything just to keep someone else from feeling uncomfortable. Your boss will get over it. She will probably see her discomfort as her problem, rather than your pushiness. Find out as much as you can about the budgetary process. You may be surprised at what you are told. You may learn that your boss knows little more than you do. She may even make a counteroffer just to stop your line of questioning.

It is possible that someone else in the corporate hierarchy makes decisions about your salary. This is not unusual. Try to find out how much leeway your manager has. Find out what she does to appropriate additional funds for specific salaries. For example, does she have to meet with someone to go over every performance review she writes and then recommend a raise, justifying every penny? Does she simply recommend a raise and get what she wants? To what extent does she determine your income? You may assume that she holds the purse strings when the decision is out of her hands. On the other hand, you may assume the decision is mandated by someone else, when your boss calls all the shots.

If someone else makes the decisions, then ask your boss to approach that person. Discuss how to do this with her. If possible, you and she together should approach the decision-making person or group of people with the justification for your raise. The second-best option would be to have you plead your own case, with your manager paving the way. The worst case, yet probably the most common, would be for your boss to approach the powers that be with your request and try to secure a raise for you. If that is the choice, ask to be present when your boss goes to the budget board, or wherever she has to go. It might seem scary, but remember what is at stake. You don't know exactly what she will say or how. You have your priorities, and she has hers. You also don't know what kind of negotiator she is. She may welcome your presence. In some cases, bringing you along would put her in a bad light. If you cannot be there, prepare your boss to act in your best interests.

You are probably not accustomed to telling your boss what to do, but you can make suggestions by asking questions. Ask your boss what time of day and which day of the week would be best to negotiate this kind of thing. She may want to combine your request with some other business she needs to discuss. Ask when your manager thinks it would best fit into the agenda. Ask which of your accomplishments she will mention first, second, third. Ask what objections she thinks will be raised. Discuss her answers to those objections. Asking for a raise is your job. In this case your boss is doing the job for you, so it becomes your job to prepare her.

## *No One Else Makes That Much*

Suppose you ask for a raise and your manager says, "No one else at your level makes that much." This may or may not be true, but keep in mind that it might very well be a negotiating strategy. Many women find it difficult to overcome this objection because we want things to be fair.

Your first thought may be, "Who am I to ask for more than everyone else makes?" Remember, you are asking for a raise because you deserve it. Your contributions to the department are important. Turn the fairness argument to your advantage. "Clearly, this company is committed to paying fair compensation to good people." Ask the salary range for people in your position. If you are already at the top, don't give up. You may have responsibilities not assigned to those around you. Perhaps your position has not been designated accurately. "I contributed a great deal to the most recent marketing piece. I'm sure you agree that this was an expansion of my current position."

Don't assume that everyone in the same position makes the same, or even similar, pay. Don't assume that any discrepancy is based on seniority. Too often we think the people who work in a position the longest make the most money, but the opposite might be true.

If additional salary is out of the question, ask for a bonus. Sometimes a bonus is easier to give because it is not an ongoing commitment. You may assume bonuses are not given to people at your job level because you have never received one. Maybe you just need to ask.

## *That's a Big Raise*

Now to a third objection you might hear when you ask for a raise: "That's a lot more than you currently make." Your long-term goal should be to change jobs, because any position usually remains in the same pay range, no matter how long we do it.

Remember that it is your employer's job to keep costs down, including your salary. Try a response that will elicit objections you can deal with: "I'm sure you want people around here to earn what they deserve" or "Don't you agree that my performance warrants the new salary?"

Decide in advance how much money you want. If you want a $4,000 raise, ask for $6,000 more. Ask for the amount in terms of your total pay, rather than focusing on the amount of the increase. "I request that my salary be raised to $38,000." Your boss may not know offhand how much you currently make. If you ask for a 30% increase, it may sound like a whole lot more.

Know ahead of time what you are willing to give up and what you are willing to accept. You may be asked to give up overtime pay. You may be asked to accept more responsibility. Try not to be taken by surprise.

You may be thrown a curve ball, such as, "We haven't hired anyone to replace Sheila. Do you want to take on her duties, in addition to yours, to justify a raise?" You are not required to come up with an answer to that kind of request immediately. It is perfectly acceptable to respond, "I hadn't thought of that possibility. I would like to have the chance to think about it and discuss it with you later." While this might have been thrown at you as a negotiating strategy, you might be able to write a new job description for your job as well as Sheila's, get the job done, and earn 50% more. Don't expect to be able to figure that out on the spot.

After being refused a raise, women too often see no alternative other than to threaten to leave the company. Threatening to quit your job might get you the same kind of response as a 30-year-old man who threatens to move out of his parent's home. You might be shown directly to the door. Even if your boss begs you to stay, you will lose credibility and be taken less seriously in the future. If you have a legitimate offer for another job, use it as a bargaining chip. If you have no such offer, don't invent one. Negotiate, negotiate, negotiate, but do not give the ultimatum of quitting.

## *Keep Your Ears Open*

In negotiating, none of our arguments will work if we don't listen to what is being said. Listen carefully, and don't try to formulate your response as the other person is talking. Rephrase what you have heard, and repeat it to the speaker, verifying that what you heard is what was intended. This may seem redundant, but you would be surprised how often we misunderstand one another. Do not judge what the speaker has to say in mid-sentence. Wait until the speaker is done before you make any assumption or evaluation. This is much easier if you are relaxed rather than tense.

As you listen, avoid nodding your head in agreement. This thoughtful nodding is a common habit of women to show that we are listening and understand what is being said, and it serves us well in many situations. In negotiations, such nodding can put you at a disadvantage, since the other person may read it as a sign that you agree with what is being said.

You may believe that you are never in a position to negotiate in business, so what good are all these rules? Let's make up an example to illustrate how there tactics might be used by you and against you.

## *Your Brilliant Idea*

As a secretary in a sales department, you see an opportunity to begin a career change that will also increase the effectiveness of your department. You decide that too much guesswork is involved in the marketing of your products.

Here's your idea: You see a position for someone who could determine where your market actually is, who is currently buying your product line and who is not, and what kinds of items customers will need in the future. You want to spend your time talking to salespeople, customers, and prospects, as well as studying records of orders. Some of these steps may sound obvious, but you would be surprised how many companies do not take the time to gather this data and use it.

You come up with the idea and then keep it to yourself. The last thing you want is for someone else to propose your idea before you do.

Next you start to gather information. If you ask casually, you will be surprised how much information you can get from people without making them suspicious. Your salespeople may have a feel for how much advertising is falling on deaf ears. You might have conversations with key customers already, and you could ask them questions such as how they originally learned about your company's product line.

Then you arrange for a negotiating session with the head of the sales department. For the sake of this example, we'll assume the sales manager is a man.

At best, as you prepare to meet with him, you arm yourself with figures on anticipated increases in sales figures, their impact on the bottom line for your department, a complete list of your responsibilities and salary requirements, and a justification of how you got all these figures.

At the least, you develop clear ideas about how to describe the new position, including the type of information you would provide that is currently unavailable and recommendations about what to do with this information. Don't give up on the idea just because you can't financially justify it before you begin. If you can sell the idea, someone will be able to help you justify it financially. Know what you have and what you need, so if asked, you can explain that you thought about a certain piece of information even though it was unavailable to you. Anticipate that the other person may try to end the discussion before it begins: "Fine, why don't you find out more about this, and then we can discuss it later?" Make sure you have all the information you have access to, or you will be asked to prepare further.

Let's say the person you want to approach, the sales department manager, is your boss's manager. The military-like structure of a corporation dictates that you approach your boss first. If you feel certain that your boss would be counterproductive to your efforts, go around her. Do this carefully to avoid creating resentment and making your current job more difficult.

One way to do this is to wait until your boss is out of town – not just busy or unavailable for a time, but physically gone. Tell the sales manager you would like to schedule a meeting to present some data that you have compiled and know he will find interesting. If he tells you to wait until your boss is back, say something like, "I know you will be the final decision-maker, and I would like an opportunity to present this to you." If necessary, try quoting some impressive figures to get the attention you need. You might even have to explain why you don't want your boss there. "I believe my manager sees me strictly as a secretary, since I have worked in that capacity for so long. I would like to be considered for an entirely new position, and I can show you how it will directly benefit this department financially." If you still don't get anywhere, don't take it personally. Tell the sales manager you will set up a meeting with your boss, and you expect him to attend the since he will be in on the decision. Do not ask if he would like to be there.

If all efforts to bypass your boss fail, schedule a presentation to several people including your boss. Send a memo to your boss, with a copy to her boss and anyone else who is involved. This will keep your manager from promising to invite her boss but not following through on it.

If you believe this position should be in another department, go as high up the corporate ladder as you can. Make an appointment with those people who are in a position to make a decision on your proposal. Women usually do not have direct contact with these people, so we allow our managers to plead our case. This may be appropriate in day-to-day matters, but would not be acceptable in this example.

## *Come Across Well*

Be sure to practice at home. If you are not used to speaking in front of a group of people, you will need to practice your presentation even more. It is necessary to project confidence and competence. Much can be accomplished with the right delivery. Be sure to guard against speaking too softly or rapidly, trailing off at the end of a sentence, or ending a sentence as if it were a question instead of a statement.

Approach the head of the department when you are ready to schedule the presentation.

## *Give it Your Best Shot*

The fear of losing what we have is a stronger motivator than that of gaining something new. You should begin by making your audience feel the pain of continuing to do things the way they have: new products are not available when needed and you are losing sales to competition. These sales often represent lost future sales, as customers begin to develop loyalty to your competitors. Money is being spent on advertising directed at those who would not buy, no matter what, or to those who represent a lower profit margin. This same advertising dollar should be targeted to high-volume, repeat customers. The problem? Your company doesn't even know who these customers are. Most companies operate in a competitive environment. Bring up matters that affect everyone and impact the company's profits, such as the competition's products, delivery schedule, prices, and advertising, as much as possible. If you can show how you will make your company more competitive, it will add power to your presentation.

## *Tactics*

Prepare yourself for negotiating by examining the following 30 negotiating tactics from Suzanne Lainson,[2] along with my suggestions for applying the tactics in this example. Some are tactics you should learn to use. Any and all are tactics that others may use against you. It is important to be aware of a few tactics you can use, as well as what might be coming at you.

---

2. Reprinted by permission of The Putnam Publishing Group from CRASH COURSE: The Instant MBA by Suzanne Lainson. Copyright © 1985 by Suzanne Lainson and The Stonesong Press, Inc.

If you can simply recognize a negotiating tactic and no more, you can more easily deal with it.

Lainson's 30 Negotiating Tactics

| Lainson's Tactics | My Suggestions for Using the Tactics |
|---|---|
| **1. Try to gain an advantage over the opposition by planting your ideas in their minds before they reach the negotiating table.** | Put a question in the memo which reminds your guests of their commitment to attend your presentation. Ask whether they know how many people on the mailing list for your company's promotional literature are potential customers, or whether they know what percentage of your customers corporations with sales revenues of $30-40 million. |
| **2. Try to catch them off-guard by doing what you want and then announcing it at the start of negotiations.** | Analyze the records you work with every day to compile data on what kinds of people are buying your products, how often, and how much. Surprise them with your opening statement: "Only 20% of our customers order products more than once a year, but we send out catalogs twice a month to everyone. Each catalog costs $1.75 for printing and mailing, plus our handling costs. If we mailed catalogs only twice a year to the other 80% of our customers, we would save $57,560 per year without dramatically affecting overall sales." |

Lainson's 30 Negotiating Tactics

| Lainson's Tactics | My Suggestions for Using the Tactics |
|---|---|
| **3. Try to use your first-strike capability by hitting them with an ultimatum rather than an offer to talk.** | In our example, I wouldn't recommend the use of an ultimatum. Keep this in mind for a situation where you already have some power. (A good example of using this tactic effectively might be a case where you have invented a product and you threaten to sell it to a competitor.) |
| **4. Try to force them into agreeing with you quickly by taking immediate action against them, rather than waiting until negotiations are set up.** | Prepare yourself to recognize this tactic coming at you, to throw you off course: "If you are so unsatisfied with your current position, perhaps you should look elsewhere for employment." You could respond: "The real issue is not my level of satisfaction, but an opportunity for the company to use my skills more productively." |

Lainson's 30 Negotiating Tactics

| Lainson's Tactics | My Suggestions for Using the Tactics |
|---|---|
| **5. Try to ensure success in the negotiations by reducing the areas of disagreement.** | Let's say your audience agrees that the proposed job is necessary, but they disagree with your ideas about the specific responsibilities. You can minimize the disagreement by saying, "All right, let's concentrate on how we can implement this job and save the job description for later."<br><br>Be on the lookout for savvy negotiators who will try to focus on unimportant differences as a distraction. Recognize this as nothing more than a tactic and don't let them do it! "I think we all agree that the size of my office is a relatively minor issue, which can be resolved once we all agree on the major facets of this proposal." |
| **6. Attempt to gain control of the negotiations by dealing with one issue at a time.** | In any group discussion, the conversation can easily flit from one thing to another. Someone may be using this tactic to keep the meeting in a state of confusion. Make a written agenda to follow. If the conversation begins to drift, say, "Let's resolve this issue before we move on to that one. We'll be getting to that later." Do not move from one item to the next until it seems logical to you. Move on when you are satisfied that all agree on how to resolve the current issue. |

Lainson's 30 Negotiating Tactics

| Lainson's Tactics | My Suggestions for Using the Tactics |
| --- | --- |
| **7. Begin by asking for everything you want in hopes that they'll agree to at least a few of your demands.** | Have a clear idea of what you want. In this example, it might be the new job title, with full leeway on how to get the results you want. If they ask what you are willing to settle for, don't tell them. They are there to negotiate, and you should be also. You can bet they won't be telling you too early what they are willing to offer. With several people present, I don't suggest you bring up the subject of salary. If one of them brings it up, you should ask if it is appropriate to negotiate salary with a group. |
| **8. Begin by asking for a great deal in order to overwhelm them.** | Begin by requesting an entire department, with your own staff. Be careful how you phrase this, or you could be laughed out of the room. "Clearly, this position warrants an entire department, but we can decide today where to start." |
| **9. Ask for the opposite of what you really want on the assumption that they will respond contrarily.** | This tactic works well with eight-year-olds. If your guests are people with mentalities of eight-year-olds, you could describe the need and then say, "I know what needs to be done, but I'm not interested in a position like that." Don't use this tactic unless you can anticipate a contrary response. |

### Lainson's 30 Negotiating Tactics

| Lainson's Tactics | My Suggestions for Using the Tactics |
|---|---|
| **10. Try to create momentum in your favor by beginning with the demands you can most easily win.** | If you present it right, you will probably get agreement on the fact that the function you propose is needed. From there, propose the creation of an entirely new position to fit the need. Next, explain how you would be best to fit the bill. Then you can move on to the more difficult battles, such as the job description and appropriate compensation. This tactic usually comes naturally for women, since we love to see everyone agree. |
| **11. Be vague about what you want to keep them from developing a counter-strategy.** | I don't recommend this tactic. In this case, they might decide you haven't done your homework. Don't be surprised if they are vague with you: "That sounds like a great idea. We'll discuss it at a later date." Your response: "This won't happen unless we establish some definite steps to take." |
| **12. Offer them something you know they want in return for what you want.** | Suppose you know they would want you to continue compiling the monthly budgeting report. You could offer to do this, as long as they agree to relieve you of all other current duties. Listen during the negotiations to determine what they want, and don't offer something that is meaningless to them. |

Lainson's 30 Negotiating Tactics

| Lainson's Tactics | My Suggestions for Using the Tactics |
|---|---|
| **13. Offer to make concessions in areas that are in fact of little concern to you.** | Know ahead of time what you are willing to give up first, second, and third. Otherwise, the emotion of the moment and the negotiating skills of your audience may confuse you into making the wrong choices. Let's say you want to insist on a good salary, but you think you can do without a secretary. Offer to do the job without a secretary for awhile, to conserve costs. |
| **14. Create false demands solely for the purpose of giving them up as a trade-off.** | Think of false demands that you can easily do without: a private office, a separate budget, or a personal assistant. Your offer to "sacrifice" these demands can lead your audience to believe they have gotten something.<br><br>Expect them to make false demands of you, too. They might claim budget restrictions as an excuse to insist that you continue performing your existing duties for the next six months. |

Lainson's 30 Negotiating Tactics

| Lainson's Tactics | My Suggestions for Using the Tactics |
| --- | --- |
| **15. Let them think they've won and then ask for a small concession.** | Let's say your whole scheme falls on deaf ears. They don't even understand the need for the proposed position, let alone see you in it. Ask if you could pursue the issue in addition to your normal responsibilities. Tell them it will help the sales force and you are truly interested in market research. Your true interest may not be possible at this company, but this experience will help you develop your resume. |
| **16. Let them think it's in their best interests to do what you want.** | Focus their attention on the figures you have prepared to show how this position will impact profit. The more quantitative information you have, the more power you have in this negotiation. Of course, say nothing of how the position may help you.<br><br>Using this tactic will serve you well in any negotiation and in business practices generally. |
| **17. Suggest that you represent a great deal of power in order to intimidate them.** | You should probably save this tactic for the board room, when you get there.<br><br>In this example, you have little power except the information you have collected. |

| Lainson's 30 Negotiating Tactics | |
|---|---|
| **Lainson's Tactics** | **My Suggestions for Using the Tactics** |
| **18. Bring powerful or influential people with you to bolster your image of strength.** | Don't forget this one. Women often hesitate to bother others or feel certain of the need to do it alone. Before the presentation, think of impressive people you might try to win over ahead of time. Speak to them about what you expect, and invite them to attend. Be sure they understand their role. Don't select people who turn into butter when asked to make requests to upper management.<br><br>If it is simply impossible or impractical to have others there, quote them during your presentation: "Ed Lawrence said he could increase sales by 20% if his sales force could concentrate on our high-volume buyers." Or: "Jack Thomas said he would love to know how many of our customers are going to convert to high-pressure systems in the next two years." |

Lainson's 30 Negotiating Tactics

| Lainson's Tactics | My Suggestions for Using the Tactics |
|---|---|
| **19. Let others represent you at the negotiations so they can say things that you might refrain from saying because it could hurt or weaken your image.** | In this example, the sales manager might be the perfect one to make a presentation to justify the need for the position and the reasons you are the best one for the job. Personality differences can get in the way of logical business decisions. If you can gain more power by having someone else suggest you are right for the spot, do it that way. Be sure to prime the person who will represent you. Rehearse, discuss, and rehearse again. Without you there, the entire focus could change and you might never know. Use this strategy only if nothing else makes sense. Don't stay away just because you are uncomfortable at the thought of being there. |
| **20. Make demands you know they can't meet and will back away from to show your aggressive position.** | Maybe you know they cannot possibly give you a private office because there is no space. Present that as a condition of this plan up front, knowing you will back away later. |

Lainson's 30 Negotiating Tactics

| Lainson's Tactics | My Suggestions for Using the Tactics |
|---|---|
| **21. Force them to drop out of the negotiations by escalating your demands far beyond any point they are prepared to meet.** | In this example, this tactic will probably not work for you. They, not you, are the final decision-makers, so you really don't want them to back out of the negotiations. Be aware of this one coming your way, though. They may suggest that you assume all new duties along with current ones at your current salary, hoping you will back down. If you remember that this is only a negotiating tactic, you might respond: "I'm sure that by the time we leave this room today, you will be able to recognize the extent of this new responsibility and its impact on the bottom line. You will appreciate the need for someone devoting full attention to the job, rather than just fitting it in." |
| **22. Change your tactics unexpectedly to throw them off-guard.** | As an example, you could skip from dealing with one issue at a time to creating false demands. Do not change tactics, however, if you are making progress with your current approach. If you are getting agreement, don't try to throw anyone off-guard. If you meet resistance, remember you are negotiating. |

Lainson's 30 Negotiating Tactics

| Lainson's Tactics | My Suggestions for Using the Tactics |
|---|---|
| **23. Have a secret plan you can exercise at the last minute if necessary.** | Your secret plan might be to tell them about an offer you received for a similar position elsewhere. You prefer to stay where you are, but your last-ditch effort can be resigning and moving on. They just might reconsider. If not, you have lost nothing. Of course, don't fabricate an offer you have not received – it is too easy to call your bluff. |
| **24. Mislead them by bluffing or distorting the facts.** | Save this tactic for another time. Facts are your ally in this example; distorting the facts will discredit you and ruin your position. To overstate the impact on profit, for example, would only make you look suspicious or even stupid. However, someone may try to use this tactic on you: "I know that 25% of last year's orders came from stainless steel customers." If you know this is not true, say so. Just because it was said by some hot-shot, doesn't make it true. |

Lainson's 30 Negotiating Tactics

| Lainson's Tactics | My Suggestions for Using the Tactics |
|---|---|
| **25. Drag out the negotiations in hopes of wearing them down.** | How many times have you given in, just because you were worn out or needed to get something else done? They might use this on you: "Don't you have to pick up your daughter? Maybe we should continue this discussion another time."<br><br>Try not to let the meeting end without resolution. If it does, set a definite time for the next meeting and list the goals you want to accomplish at that time. Summarize what you have resolved so far and clarify any unsettled matters. "We all agree that such a function is crucial to the success of this department. We acknowledge that I am an excellent candidate for the position. We will meet on Tuesday from 9 to 10 a.m. to discuss whether a new position can be created and what the details will be." Specify a time frame with a clear starting and ending time, so that everyone involved can allocate the time, with no excuse for cutting it short. |

## Lainson's 30 Negotiating Tactics

| Lainson's Tactics | My Suggestions for Using the Tactics |
| --- | --- |
| **26. Weaken their resolve by saying very little.** | Once you have presented your proposal, quit talking. Give them time to discuss it, unless the conversation takes a negative turn.<br><br>This is a tactic that may well be used on you. Everyone might keep quiet to put you on the spot. If you meet with little response, ask very specific questions: "Steve, do you agree that we are unaware how many of our customers are moving to high-pressure systems?" If he disagrees, ask how many customers are making this move and how he knows. If the answer contradicts information that you have, say so. Don't assume he knows simply because he is in a decision-making position. This silence act can really catch you off-guard. Don't just keep talking, because you might give away more than you should. Get some response. You might try asking, "Can I assume from your silence that we should go ahead with my plan?" That just might be the case. |

| Lainson's 30 Negotiating Tactics | |
|---|---|
| **Lainson's Tactics** | **My Suggestions for Using the Tactics** |
| **27. Leave the negotiations unexpectedly in order to throw them off guard and to suggest your lack of interest.** | Let's say they appear very interested in your idea, but they refuse to consider you for the position. You might offer to leave the room to allow them to discuss it. Be aware of someone throwing you off-guard by suddenly leaving: "I have an important call to make." If this happens, ask exactly when the person will return and whether the group should wait or reschedule the meeting. This is also a reason to establish a certain time frame for the meeting and make sure you keep your presentation within that time frame. |
| **28. Attempt to pressure them into dealing with you by refusing to discuss the matter much longer.** | This one will surely come your way: "It sounds like a great idea, Sally. We'll give it every consideration." To prevent this, begin your presentation by saying: "I have a proposal that will impact the success of this company. I will explain it to you, and then I would like a decision on my proposal today." Although this may sound like strong language, asking only that they listen to you will almost certainly get you nowhere. |

| Lainson's Tactics | My Suggestions for Using the Tactics |
|---|---|
| **29. Depend on several different people with several different styles to present your case, alternating back and forth between them as suits the discussion.** | Bring as many allies as you can. If feasible, give them a specific part of the presentation to give, even if you authored it all. There is always strength in numbers – don't hog the show. |
| **30. If you've lost most of your demands, suggest that they grant you at least one or two as a measure of good faith.** | If they have turned you down cold, take advantage of the fact that they may feel somewhat guilty. "As a measure of good faith, how about letting me talk to major customers when they receive their invoice? I can ask if the product is satisfactory and try to get them in a conversation about their future direction." You may be swamped with work, but don't forget the goal of developing your resume. In future job interviews, such contact with customers can only help you. |

This example is hypothetical, but it may be similar to opportunities you have to negotiate. Try to see negotiations going on around you. Try to recognize the negotiating tactics that others are using with you. Rather than allowing the negotiating process to intimidate you, begin to see it as a normal part of business and life.

While women may not know how to negotiate, we sometimes knock ourselves out to stand our ground. This may only serve to make us appear unreasonable and inflexible, rather than strong and assertive.

Consider what kind of negotiator you are. You may decide you are too wishy-washy, simply accepting what comes your way instead of negotiating. You may decide that you are too stoic and rigid, unable to change your position. You probably find yourself somewhere in between. Wake up to the negotiating around you, jump in, and become a participant in the process.

*"...Job statistics indicate that the average person changes careers three to five times during a lifetime."*[1]

CHAPTER 8

# Where's the Work?

Countless of us look for a job without a clear idea of what kind of work we want. We expect the human resources director somehow to determine our strengths and put us in the correct position. Then we expect our boss to recognize our abilities and promote us.

I guarantee that for every 100 companies where you say, "I would like a job, and I don't really know what kind of work I prefer, but I'm a hard worker and I can learn fast," at least 95 will consider you for "female jobs" only.

Too many women are willing to settle for this decision. We are comfortable in a task-oriented environment. We are surrounded by women who follow many of the rules we have learned. We are convinced that we will learn what we need to know and be promoted from where we are. Often we are promoted, which only reinforces our expectations. What we don't realize is that we are stuck driving in the slow lane, while others have moved into the passing lane. Somehow we know the difference is reflected in our paychecks.

1. Coxford, Lola M. (1989). *Resume Writing Made Easy* (p. 68). Scottsdale, AZ: Gorsuch Scarisbrick.

## *Starting Lane*

Let's say you have no formal education in business and no work experience. Where do you start? Suppose you apply to a company and say nothing about what you want, or you make obscure comments about yourself: "I like people," or "I'm good at detail." As a woman, you might be placed in an administrative job, with a PC on your desk, and a list of tasks to perform.

Where would a man start if he applied at the same company with no experience and obscure career goals? He might well begin in the mail room. Maybe administration jobs pay more money or you have better working conditions than the mail clerk, so you think you have the better deal. The big difference, however, is that he is beginning a male career path, while you are now on the first step of a female career path. You are in two entirely different lanes.

In deciding what we want, women usually have two disadvantages. First, our positions in the corporate world typically keep us from being exposed to the overall picture and prevent us from seeing other opportunities. We often have no idea of what most other people in our company do for a living. Second, we are guilty of limiting our focus to what we know or, worse, what interests us. We assume that unless we already have knowledge or interest in a field, then we cannot learn to do the work or love the job. Yet most successful men and women in this country happened upon their field almost by accident. They began and continued a career without necessarily planning each step, but they looked for and grabbed at the opportunities around them.

Maybe you know what you don't want, but not what you do want. You can recite all the reasons you couldn't possibly perform one of those high-profile, risk-oriented jobs. It's time to wake up and realize that you're an adult now. Open your eyes and mind to new possibilities. People all around you are trying things they are unsure of, fumbling and making mistakes, and getting paid quite well. Don't wait around for some golden opportunity to slap you in the face. Quit making a list of what you don't want to do. Start to dig up what's out there.

## *Finding a Job is a Job*

Allow yourself to take the time and trouble to search for a good opportunity. Begin today, but don't expect to change careers tomorrow or next month. From now on, you will be developing and working on a career plan. You will be somewhere on this career course for the rest of your working life, so don't take it lightly. Take control.

Successful people might apply to 500 different companies to get 50 job interviews and choose among five job offers. Many women apply to five or 10 companies, have a couple of interviews, get rejected, and give up. We stay where we are, not for lack of opportunity, but for lack of trying. We become discouraged too easily, lacking entitlement and deciding that we aren't qualified anyway. We view rejection from a job not as the employer's loss, but as confirmation of our lack of self-worth, our lack of qualifications. Convinced that we are lucky to have any job at all, we stay where we are.

It may seem easier to stay where you are with the pay you have than face the rejection that comes with job-hunting. However, it is much harder to live on a low income than a higher one. Each year that you continue to work for low pay, your life is harder than it potentially could be. Yes, changing careers is hard, but you have done many hard things in your life. It may be time to do another one.

If you are currently out of work, it may seem like a logical time to change your course. However, you may not have the luxury of time. Certainly, investigate every high-paying opportunity you can uncover, but you may need to take the first job offered just to pay the rent. Don't be discouraged, you are not the first to do what you had to do. Wear a business suit every day to your new job, and keep looking around for another opportunity. Once you have an income, you can take the necessary time to change lanes. You may find that the job you accepted was a better opportunity than you thought. You may change companies again within a few weeks or months.

It was suggested that I provide a list of "male track" careers here. I could then guide you from one job to another. I could tell you that if you are good at a certain female job, you could transfer your skills to a specific male job. This would make the choice less complicated and help you avoid making a mistake. Perhaps this is what you would like – some careful guidance to erase the confusion.

There are several problems with this approach. To begin with, I don't want to erase the confusion and make the job less complicated. Finding a career you like is complicated. We need to face the uncertainty of the adult working world.

Some of us love having someone tell us exactly what to do. This takes the responsibility off our shoulders and makes someone else accountable for the decision. It also keeps us childlike, however, and unable to think for ourselves. It keeps our pay excruciatingly low. The jobs that require the toughest decisions and make us most accountable for those decisions pay the most money. We need to get used to making decisions when the outcome is unknown. We need to become accustomed to taking the heat when our decisions are incorrect. We need to learn to defend ourselves when we are right.

The "skills" you need may simply be a new attitude toward taking risks, working as a team member, negotiating, projecting confidence, and focusing on results instead of tasks. If you can project confidence and develop an orientation to the company's bottom line, you will be considered for many job opportunities. Your education did not end when you finished school. You can learn what you need to know to get the job done.

Even if I thought it were a good idea, I could not tell you what kind of job you would do well or what you would enjoy. A job is much more than performing tasks and accomplishing results. The people where you work usually affect your success and satisfaction more than your job description. I have worked for enough companies to know that every office environment is different. Maybe all the women in your office are forbidden opportunities; there may be a pattern of talking down to or even sexually harassing women. Maybe your office environment is conducive to career women, but not regular women. Try to take a realistic survey of the company you currently work for, but don't beat your head against a brick wall for too long. Look both inside and outside your company walls.

## *What Do You Want?*

Women go to career counselors to determine what kind of work would be best for them. Harragan believes that career counselors and vocational guidance people almost unanimously accept the premise that women are deficient. They encourage us to compensate for our deficiencies by returning to school for additional courses or degrees. At the other end of the spectrum, career guidance takes the form of ceaseless probing into the woman's personal attributes. Can she lead others? Can she make decisions? Is she willing to sacrifice her home life for her job? Has she analyzed her patterns of success, her assertiveness, her reasons for working?

This kind of soul-searching to discover the perfect career can waste time and cause confusion. We all have our own ways of handling different aspects of our lives. Some men and women are successful in their careers, but a flop at other things. The same person who makes snap business decisions can shop all over town before making up his mind on a cantaloupe. All of us are assertive in some circumstances, and painfully shy in others. I know people who are immaculate housekeepers, but whose offices look like a battlefield. Accurate descriptions of our personal selves may have nothing to do with our business potential. Beware of this kind of self-evaluation as it applies to a career; it may not apply to your career at all.

Don't assume you have to pursue something that interests you. Most people had no particular interest in their line of work until they started doing it and learning it. Keep your hobbies as hobbies, and see what kind of opportunities exist in the job market.

So what do you do? I recommend these two steps:

1. Investigate everything, leaving no stone unturned. Accept the fact that you don't know exactly what kind of work you want, and don't worry about it. Keep an open mind.
2. Project the image of knowing exactly what you want.

Before you decide this is impossible, consider that this is exactly what most other job hunters are doing right now. It is dangerous to narrow your focus, especially when you are contemplating a major career change. You owe it to yourself to look into all kinds of opportunities. It is also important to appear certain about what you want. You will never land a good job if you seem unclear about your chosen path.

We eliminate thousands of opportunities that we might love just because something about a job seems unfamiliar or the job doesn't sound like fun. Is there anything about your current job that is not fun? Is any job perfect for any person? Of course not. It is the nature of work that nearly every job offers satisfaction, frustration, stress, boredom, and income. The same job can be a lot more fun, however, when it pays $80,000 a year than when it pays $10,000. Broaden your focus, and look at every possibility. You will be amazed at the ways people make a living. You might also be amazed at what they are paid.

Your next job and every job thereafter are jobs on a career path. The next job you take is important, but it does not have to be perfect. I have seen women sit by instead of grabbing an opportunity that would lead to bigger and better things because it wasn't exactly what they wanted. To hold out for the prime slot is professional suicide. Remember that women have higher expectations for their work and lower expectations for their pay. You may or may not have to start at the bottom of your career path, but get on the right path. It is not always a direct line, but there are a lot of pleasant surprises along the way.

## *Start Looking*

Now that you are thinking seriously about a change, opportunities will become more evident. Don't follow a career plan just because it seems to make sense to you; follow one that is normally followed by males. It may seem that a job as secretary to the president could provide good training for the job of president, but it will not lead to that position. Find out what others have done and are doing. Don't make assumptions based on your own exposure to the work force.

So, where's the work?

You have a lot more options than you think. Basically, they fall into five categories.

1. Stay with the company where you currently work and find an opportunity that exists.

2. Stay with your current employer and create an opportunity for yourself.
3. Change companies and fill an opening elsewhere.
4. Create a position in another company and convince them to hire you to fill it.
5. Start your own company.

Now is the time to explore these possibilities simultaneously. In this book, we will concentrate on the first four options. We will not go into detail on starting your own business, many other publications can help you with that process.

## *Your Current Employer*

There are many reasons to stick with the company where you now work. You know the people and the overall philosophy of the corporation. You probably know much more about the political structure than you think, and you know quite a bit about the flow of work. You recognize the flaws in the system, from your vantage point. It is logical to find out what you can offer your current employer. It may be possible to move into an existing position in a male job track or create a position for yourself.

Make a list of the various jobs around you. Categorize each as a "male" or "female" job. This may be hard for some jobs, but try to do it anyway. Also, try to categorize them as line or staff positions. Pretty soon, you will have a long list and a better idea of who earns what, just by making a list. Get an organizational chart, which names the titles from CEO down. Some charts list individual names and others list only titles. You may have to look at several organizational charts, one for each department you are interested in. Remember that you do not have to have a goal of becoming president of the company to have the ambition to move into a male career path and earn more money.

Don't assume that everyone with the same title earns the same pay. There may be several vice presidents. You can be sure that those on the line are paid better than those on staff. Even if you don't aspire to the vice presidential level, you will be much better off working for someone who is already on the fast track. The highest-paid vice presidents usually have the highest-paid subordinates because their departments are considered more vital to the company's bottom line. Typically these are line positions.

## *Ask Others About Their Jobs*

Talk to some people in your company about what they do for a living. You probably know a lot of them, even if you don't know exactly what they do. Specifically, try to talk to women who are in male-dominated career paths. If that's not possible, talk to some men in jobs that appeal to you. Ask what their jobs are like and how they accomplish their goals. Find out what experience they had before coming to your company. If you believe you don't have the "qualifications" for their jobs, ask what jobs in your company could lead to jobs like theirs.

If you decide you want to pursue a career like theirs, go a step further. If you can confide in these people, find out who to talk to about a job in their camp. Ask them to keep the conversation confidential, even if you are embarrassed to do so. Explain that your boss doesn't know about your ambitions just now.

If you know some people who can help you gain a new position, ask if they think you would do a good job. If they try to help you, listen carefully to what they say. They know more about the politics of the situation than you. They know more about what it takes to get the job than you.

Let's say Sally suggests that you call a man who is vice president of marketing about a position as an analyst. Let's say you don't want to call him, so you decide to write him a memo. Sally knows that this man never reads his memos, but asks his secretary to scan them. She knows he wants a certain level of assertiveness in employees that a memo will not demonstrate. If you want to deviate from Sally's suggestions, tell her exactly what you want to do. Many a job could have been landed if people had only listened to those whom they asked for advice. If these people don't want to help you, however, don't give up. They may just be busy or even feel threatened.

Take a look at the corporate climate of your company. How do you compare to others in your industry? How do the opportunities in your industry compare to others? By their nature, some industries are more dynamic than others, offering more opportunities for everyone. We sometimes assume that a company is a better place to work because a lot of people have heard of it or the offices are nice. Get real.

Also beware of having this perception of companies as you interview. Some of the highest-paid women in this country work for companies you have never heard of. All companies are good for some people and bad for others.

Don't limit yourself to departments or companies that appear to have good opportunities for women. If there are many women and very few men in a certain job, the women may receive very low pay, even if they all seem to be career women. Look for opportunities that are good, and don't assume your gender will be the main consideration. Whatever you do, remember the distinction between line and staff.

As you look to move within the company, protocol requires that your immediate supervisor or manager be aware and supportive of any move you make within the organization. This may or may not be realistic. You know your situation best. Don't tell your boss tomorrow that you will be looking for another job unless you expect your boss to sit down and help you do so. It may be best to wait until you have a better understanding of what you want to pursue.

You might have to bypass your manager. Often a boss doesn't know an employee is moving within the organization until the move is announced. Your manager can be a tremendous advocate, telling you whom to approach when or recommending you to a potential manager. On the other hand, your boss could work against you for various reasons. Your manager might not want to lose you, may not want to train someone else, or may simply have no interest in helping employees develop their careers.

If your company has a human resources department, you can learn a great deal about jobs in your company. These people have all the information you need on who reports to whom, what qualifications are desired for various jobs, and income ranges for any position. Some of this may be unavailable to you, but much is made available to all who ask. Some human resources staff members believe all hiring decisions are made through them, even when that rarely occurs. Be careful about confidentiality. While it is unusual, I have known people who worked in human resources and broadcasted everything they knew to the rest of the company. You know your situation. The personnel department is there for a function, so use them to gather information, but continue your own internal job search simultaneously.

If you don't want to talk to your manager and don't know who to approach, go to the vice president of the division you are interested in joining. In discussing a job change, you are better off to start as high on the corporate ladder as possible for your first conversation. A high-level executive will probably not be the one to make a hiring decision and therefore will not have to worry about denying you a job. As a result, this person may be more open and willing to offer you advice on where to start.

If this vice president refers you to someone else, be sure to follow up on that suggestion. Make an appointment and start the conversation by saying, "Edna Jones told me to speak with you."

If this vice president makes a vague comment such as, "We will sure keep you in mind if we get an opening," ask questions to clarify the next step. Such a comment could mean anything. Go ahead and ask, "What would be the best step for me to take next? I am really interested in pursuing a career in this field. I believe I have more to offer this company than any other, because I am familiar with the products, the people, and the process by which things are done. I also know some of the bottlenecks around here and how best to go around or overcome them. I would like to know if I can secure a position in our company so I can plan my career." This would drive home your interest and make it clear that you won't accept just any old job.

You may be told, "We are looking for people who are more qualified than you." Ask what those qualifications are. If it is experience in the field, ask whether anyone without that experience has ever been hired and how that person worked out. Ask what positions within the company would lead to what you want. If the qualifications include a certain educational background, ask the same questions. Do not go out and enroll in night school, thinking that this opportunity will open up when you graduate. If education is truly the issue, offer to attend night school once you have the position.

Announcing your intentions can help you avoid watching someone else get hired and hearing the manager say, "Gee, we didn't know you were interested in that position, or we would have hired you."

## *Make a Job*

As you explore possibilities that exist, see if you can identify positions that don't exist. Write your own ticket.

My friend Jackie decided that her position of national sales manager no longer fit the life-style she was after, yet she wanted to stay with the same firm and capitalize on what she had learned there. Over a period of time, she took note of things that were not getting done and how much that was potentially costing the company. She was privy to much of this information due to her position, but so were many others. She made a presentation to top management with a proposed job description to get these things done. She explained what kinds of things she sought to handle, what she believed the job would be worth, and how the company could justify it through increased revenue and decreased costs. She wrote her own ticket, including her own hours, and they bought it. They would have been fools to refuse.

Women are often in a position to see all kinds of inefficiencies, but we just sit around and complain about them. Write your own ticket, and see if you can sell it. Even if they don't take you up on it, you will have demonstrated initiative and savvy, qualities that they (and you) might not have known you have.

Each of us sees ways in which things could be improved around us. I'm sure you could easily name several ways your own job could be made more efficient! If you don't see anything worth proposing to management, talk to the people in line positions. Get to know them, and work with them if you can. You will find that they can see many ways in which your company's bottom line could be improved. Like everyone else, they are too busy doing their own jobs to propose many changes. That's where you can come in.

Once you recognize a need for improvement, and you have an idea of how to make the improvement, get as many facts as you can. These facts should be quantified in dollars – increased revenue or decreased expenses – whenever possible. Do not discuss your ideas with those around you, or you might find them taking credit for your ideas.

Although this may appear tougher than finding a position that already exists, there are certain advantages. You create the job, so you determine the goals and objectives to a certain extent. More important, others will see you as an ambitious, assertive person who knows what she wants and goes after it. Be sure to prepare a complete proposal; do not casually suggest it to anyone. Have your salary and other requirements ready, and be prepared to negotiate. Don't assume that because it is obvious to you, it must have been tried before. Maybe someone thought of it, but didn't prepare the justification needed to sell it. Writing your own ticket can be one of the fastest ways to get promoted.

## *Your Company is Not the Whole World*

As you investigate the possibilities around you, also begin to look elsewhere. If your first reaction is to reject this step, evaluate the reasons you do not want to change companies.

According to those who counsel business people, women are more apt than men to knock themselves out getting their career goals in line only at the company where they work, as if no other company existed. Yet people who move from company to company, on the average, move up faster and earn more money than those who remain with the same firm. You have a reputation where you are. It may be good or bad, or both, but it is probably a reputation as a person in a woman's job. This may be reason enough to move. It may be easier for you to build a reputation as a competent, professional career woman among people who don't know you than to change your image where you are. Moving to a different company can also change your outlook if you are trying to take yourself and your career more seriously. If you are having trouble seeing yourself as strong and competent, new surroundings may make it easier for you. The working atmosphere is entirely different from one place to another. Granted, you know what you are giving up, but you don't know what you are getting. So what? Find out as much as you can, and take the plunge. You can always change companies again if things don't work out.

If you are concerned about sacrificing a retirement program, find out exactly what you would be giving up if you left at a certain time. It is not unusual for employees to review their retirement program. Ask the human resources department what is in your account and how much is *vested*, or available if you quit now. Vesting refers to contributions made by your employer to your account. Find out what percentage becomes vested at various stages of service. For instance, you might be 75% vested after 8 years and 100% vested after 10 years. Contributions deducted from your own income are always available to you if you resign, and these funds can be credited toward a retirement account elsewhere. You might find that waiting a year could make a big difference to your retirement account. You might discover that staying six more years is necessary. If you can earn significantly more money by going to work for someone else, you can usually offset any loss you take by leaving. I am flabbergasted at the length of time many women will stick with the same lousy job at the same lousy pay and justify the decision with lousy retirement benefits. Find out exactly where you stand. Talk to an accountant if you like, but make an educated decision. Note that people who work with benefits on a regular basis have been known to speak in what sounds like a foreign language when explaining these matters. If you do not understand, say so. It is your retirement account, and you have a right to know and understand its status.

My friend Joanne kept a job with a company she hated because she had multiple sclerosis. Her disease was in remission, but she was convinced that no one else would hire her if they had to insure her. Had she interviewed elsewhere, she probably would have found another job with the coverage she needed. Many large and medium-sized corporations negotiate with insurance carriers to accept any person they hire and every member of the employee's family, regardless of existing health conditions. Another friend changed insurance carriers in the middle of a pregnancy and had no trouble getting the coverage she needed. If health insurance is a concern for you or any member of your family, don't assume that you are stuck. Also, leaving a company does not always mean losing that insurance coverage immediately. Human resources staff can tell you how to continue your coverage and how much it will cost. Health care insurance in this country is expected to change over the next few years. Right now, coverage and premiums vary dramatically, depending on where you work. Find out the facts before you drop your coverage, but it may not be impossible to make a change.

Many of us feel disloyal shopping for a job while we are working, especially if we like the people where we work. It seems kind of like shopping around to see if you can find a better husband. Remember the two definitions of loyalty, male and female. If you have ever been unexpectedly laid off, you know how much loyalty exists from corporation to employee. You owe them an honest day's work, today, and nothing else. Remember also that many women love to attach guilt to anything and everything. Sometimes guilt can make us choose right from wrong. Too often, guilt causes us to make decisions that have nothing to do with right and wrong.

Sally went to lunch with a man who was bemoaning the fact that his company spent a lot of money training women for typically male positions, only to have them quit the company to take care of families. Sally's response was, "John, men do it all the time." Men accept positions, become trained, and quit for greener pastures. Keep this in mind if you feel uneasy about accepting a position you do not intend to keep. Men – and many women – do it all the time. They are building their careers, not just doing their jobs.

You may simply feel hesitant about making a change. If this is your reason, examine it closely. None of us handles change as gracefully as we would like, but welcoming and embracing new opportunities can be a sign of maturity. Maybe you don't want to make a change just for the sake of change, but this might be exactly why you should. The same attitude that keeps you in the same company could be what is keeping you in that same dead-end job. Your image, self-image, and potential may be easier to change if you change your environment.

Generally speaking, don't change jobs unless you can change career paths. Of course, if a position similar to your current one opens up and you can double your income, you might want to consider it. As you search, many interviewers and employment counselors will encourage you to accept a position just like the one you currently have. Why? Because you are so clearly qualified, you have direct experience. You may be told there are more opportunities where you are going, you just need to get in the door and get your feet wet. If they have all these great opportunities, why don't they offer you one now? Don't get caught in the trap of accepting a low-paying female job, with a promise that you will be considered for something else once you learn the ropes. You have spent enough time learning the ropes where you are and have succeeded only in being tied up in them. You don't have to start at the top, but you do need to get into the passing lane. Make a change for the right career path.

Sometimes a job that is female-dominated in one firm is male-dominated in another. For example, if you have been working in a low-paying, dead-end, female-dominated job in customer service, don't change companies for the same situation. However, if you find a company that uses customer service as training ground for other opportunities, pays considerably more, and hires lots of men as well as women, you may want to consider making a change for the same title.

## *Create a Job Elsewhere*

Many successful people have been able to convince a corporation to create a position based on their special qualifications. If you have accomplished something unusual at your company, or watched someone else do it, you may be able to take that knowledge elsewhere. Suppose your company decided to handle repeat business through a telemarketing team, rather than the regular sales force. Find another company you believe would benefit from this process. Explain the impact of this change on handling orders much more efficiently and generating much more business for the company. Propose that you set up such a function and run it. Be sure to have a complete presentation, with as many facts and figures as possible. The advantages are clear: you write the job description, you determine the pay, at least partially, and the company sees you as an expert from the moment you are hired.

As you change companies, take care not to burn any bridges. We never know who might show up where or what they might be doing. Sometimes we are tempted to use our exit as an opportunity to set the record straight. Don't do it. Leave with grace, no matter why you are leaving. You will not be sorry.

## *Seek Possibilities*

You have begun to consider the options of finding or creating a position where you work and finding or creating a position elsewhere. Now, put several different job-finding processes in place simultaneously. Follow every job-finding route you can come up with. Finding the right job is a full-time job, as anyone will tell you. If you are currently employed, it may be harder and take longer, but you are fortunate not to be out of work. You need only one job, but the more opportunities you can find, the better your chance of landing one you like. When you sell a house, you need only one buyer, but still you try to show your home to as many potential buyers as you can. You are selling yourself now.

Ellen has a good job in a male job track. Her friend Lori came to her in tears with a rejection letter from a large, multinational company. Lori had really wanted to work for them. Ellen brought out a box full of rejection letters she had received before landing her job. You need only one job, but you will probably have to go through many possibilities to get it.

Don't rely completely on your own knowledge. Ask, read, and ask some more. If you are interested in advertising, for example, don't limit your search to advertising agencies. Many companies have advertising departments of their own. If you don't know what to do, do something. The worst thing you can do is hang around waiting for some kind of revelation to hit you about what you should do with your working life. At the very least, read about several careers and jobs. Talk to people who work in different fields. If possible, work in several until you find the best fit.

Discover what kinds of jobs exist and how people get them. If something sounds interesting to you, investigate. If you think you might be good at a certain job, you can probably learn to be. Read your local want ads, and read ads for jobs in another city where you might consider moving. In the want ads, sometimes specific qualifications are described. Remember this: companies often list qualifications for an ideal candidate but they are usually willing to interview many people without all those qualifications. They will almost assuredly hire someone who does not meet all the listed requirements. Many times educational requirements are listed, but pay attention to how these are given. "EE required" means something very different from "degree preferred."

Check the bulletin board in places where you volunteer. Susan volunteered at a hospital and found a full-time position there by doing this. Go to your local college or technical school to check the bulletin boards in various departments. There is no law against walking around a college campus and reading posted information, no matter what your education level.

Start to interview. If you are currently working, it may be difficult, but not impossible, to schedule appointments. Most employers appreciate your predicament and will interview you during your lunch time or after business hours. Don't tell anyone you work with that you are interviewing, unless you want your boss to know.

Be sure to interview for jobs that you don't want. You may be surprised at how this can help you define the type of job you want.

Maybe you see no opportunities that interest you. Schwartz explains that when we believe something is impossible, our minds go to work to prove why. When we believe something can be done, however, our minds go to work to help us find ways to accomplish it.

Put this phenomenon to work for you. Believe that you can make a good living, and your mind will help provide ways to do it. For many years, women in this country were completely excluded from certain kinds of jobs. Because it was impossible to obtain these jobs, most of us did not aspire to them. Now that the doors are unlocked, much more is possible. Viewing it as possible is the first step. It is possible not only for men and certain women, but also for you. There will be jobs you cannot get, but there are a lot more possibilities than you need in one lifetime.

## *Enlist the Help of Those Around You*

Don't try to do it all alone. Many people can help you. Some are your friends or acquaintances, and some are professionals who make their living by helping people find work.

Networking – using the help of friends, former colleagues, and others in your field – may be the best method of finding a job. According to a 1990 article in *The Wall Street Journal*, networking was used successfully by 60 percent of job-seeking clients that placement firm Manchester, Inc., surveyed over an 18- month period. Of the 351 respondents, only 17 percent used an employment agency and 15 percent answered or ran an advertisement to land a job.

Begin a network to help you look for work. Men seem to do this automatically. Women do it, too, but often we count on a network of other women, who may not have access to the jobs we want. Talk to your male friends about your career goals.

Remember to project the image of knowing what you want. It won't do to say, "I want to work with computers." Perhaps you think you don't know any men well enough to network with them. Men call each other up after 10 years of no correspondence and network for jobs. You don't need an intimate friendship to network. What you need is confidence and specific career goals. Don't ask what kinds of jobs are available. Instead, tell them what you want to pursue. "I want you to know what I'm up to, since you might hear of something from time to time." Think of men you might know from church, volunteer work, husband's friends or acquaintances, bowling teams, and so on. Be sure to include men you know from your work. Anyone you contact needs to appreciate the confidentiality of this process. You do not want to jeopardize the job you have, and may have to remind people of this. Network with the women you know who are in "male" career paths. You may be surprised how helpful they want to be. As you network for job possibilities, be free with your resume. Don't expect even good friends to memorize your credentials.

To find one job, you may have to network with scores of people. Talk to your friends, former schoolmates, and neighbors. Tell them you're job hunting, and ask for suggestions and contacts. Don't overlook anyone. Your neighbor's aunt may know someone in broadcasting or offshore drilling.

## *Employment Agencies*

One way to find a position is through employment agencies, sometimes known as headhunters. Many people have secured good jobs through employment agencies. A lot of women reject this route because they had a bad experience or don't want to pay to get a job. Many employment agencies have access to jobs you do not know about. Use them wisely, however; do not allow them to sabotage your efforts.

Employment agencies make money by charging a fee when someone they've lined up to interview is hired. When a firm uses an employment agency to help them find an employee, the hiring company decides whether or not to pay the fee associated with the search. At any given time, employment agencies will know of some openings that are fee-paid and others that are not. If you absolutely cannot pay for the service, ask to be considered only for positions that are fee-paid.

Make sure that you and your employment agency both agree about what this means. Depending on your field, you may be eliminating many possibilities. Sometimes part of the fee is paid by the employer, and you would pay the rest if you are hired. Sometimes the employee pays the fee, which is later reimbursed by the employer. Linda paid $900 to accept a position that paid considerably more than any other job she had interviewed for at the time. That was a lot of money to her in those days, but she decided it was worth it. After six months, her new employer refunded the fee to her. She stayed with the company for 10 years and had a brilliant career. Had she limited her search to fee-paid openings, she would have eliminated that opportunity.

Employment agents have a wide variety of skill levels. The most successful recruiters are very highly paid and are well respected by colleagues and employers alike. There are many at the other end also. Typically, their income is based on commissions. There is a tremendous amount of turnover, partly because the job is tough and partly because many become employment agents only to learn where the good jobs are.

Employment agents get paid when you are hired for a job, not necessarily a good job. For this reason, they might try to place you quickly in a position they can easily secure because of your experience. They may try to convince you that you are worth less income than you request, so you will settle for what they can find easily. They may have ego problems; they never earned that much money, so why should you think you are worth it?

Job-hunting is a particularly humbling experience. Keep this in mind, and do not allow any employment agent to devalue you. If you don't see eye to eye on what you are worth and what you are capable of doing, find another agent. As a matter of fact, you should be working with two or three as you look for a job on your own. It may take awhile to find two or three employment agents you like. Don't give up. Both good and bad counselors usually work in the same agency, just as good and bad hairdressers work in the same shop. They may ask that you work with them exclusively. Remember that your future is at stake, not theirs. You want to find a good job in your time frame, not theirs. This is your job search, not theirs. Knowing that you are working with other agents and on your own will help keep them on their toes. If you interview for a position with one employment agency, do not disclose the name of the company to other agencies. During your job search, call each employment counselor every day, see what they have cooking for you, ask their advice, and tell them as soon as you accept a position. After you are on the job, call your favorite employment counselors when you know of another opening in your company and tell them which person to contact about the job. You never know when you may need them again. Some agencies specialize in certain types of work, such as clerical or legal work. Agencies often run ads for jobs in the paper to attract applicants who are interested in a certain line of work. They will interview you, much like a potential employer. This is good practice, and the best counselors will help you hone your interviewing skills. Ask what they think of your responses to specific interview questions. Remember, however, that these people are not your employers. Don't just blindly follow wherever they lead.

When working with employment agents, try to be as clear as possible about what kind of work interests you. They cannot read your mind. A long list of things you would not like to do is only partially helpful.

Beware of any employment search firm that requires the applicant to pay in advance for a position. They might tell you they will make every effort to find the right job for you. They may quote you an exceptionally high income that they believe you are worth, which will be a real boost for your ego. Then they will charge you a percentage of that figure as a fee, whether they ultimately find you a position or not. Stay away from this kind of operation. Use a service that charges you or the employer only if a position is secured.

As you begin to work with employment agencies, you may be offered a job working for them. Many agencies have a lot of turnover and thus are always looking for good people. Most employment agencies have some agents who accepted a position solely to find another job for themselves. After all, who is in a better position to find out what opportunities exist and where, and what they are paying? Some of these people decide they enjoy being employment agents and stay on, either with the same agency or another. If you receive an offer, don't slough it off too quickly. It can be a good training ground for a lot of different careers. It is considered sales experience, and helps you learn to use the telephone effectively. You talk daily with decision-makers in all kinds of firms. You may enjoy this kind of work and decide to make it your career, at least for a few years. You may find another job cross your desk that you like even more. Be sure to get any agreements about pay in writing when you are hired. There is a chance you will quit before you have earned anything for the company, even if you have been paid.

## *College Recruiters and Job Fairs*

Businesses send recruiters to college campuses to hire graduates. If you went to college, no matter how long ago, call your alma mater and ask to be included in these interviews. If you live in another town, ask to be put on a mailing list of employers and interviewers.

Go to job fairs that are advertised in the paper. If you are out of work, go to all the job fairs. If you are working, be more selective.

## *Want Ads*

Whatever you do, don't forget the want ads in the newspaper. It may be true that 80 percent of jobs are not advertised, but this means that 20 percent are. You need only one job. Newspaper ads provide a way to meet employment agents who know of other opportunities. These ads can get you in the door to interview with companies who have other, unadvertised positions.

Follow up on interesting ads with a cover letter and resume. Read all the ads, not just the big ones. Some people refuse to answer ads that do not name the company, but this is often just a way for the employer to avoid a deluge of calls from employment agents. The employer and the job may be very good.

Customize your cover letter for each ad, indicating why you believe you would be good at the job. This will get easier with time, and you will be able to send similar letters to different companies. Have several resumes printed, so you can send the one which puts you in the best light for that job. Preparing cover letters and resumes should become a regular activity every Sunday afternoon (and probably evening) until you secure a position. It is important to respond to ads promptly. You should do research on a company before an interview, but it is not necessary before responding to an ad. Make sure your resume and cover letter have no typographical errors, but don't labor over them for days to get them exactly right for the job. Someone else may be hired as you are perfecting your response to a want ad.

## *A Job You Don't Want?*

Even as you look for a better opportunity, be aware that you are also developing your resume with experience. Many people accept jobs, not for the pay or prestige, but because it will be good experience for a future opportunity. I have seen men take positions, saying they intend to stay a year or so, but ready to change departments or companies with these jobs on their resumes.

Women too often stay in dead-end jobs waiting for the golden opportunity to come along, certain that we will miss it if we take a job we really don't want. The job you don't want may lead to a golden opportunity, or it may even turn out to be something you enjoy. I encourage you to make a change for the right career path, even if the first job you accept is not what you want. Your worst nightmare of a job may be a boost to your resume.

If you don't know what you want to do, begin the process of finding out what exists. You will begin to clarify your strengths and goals as you look for a new opportunity. By this time you are working on changing your attitude and your appearance. Even though it may take a while to make the change in jobs, every step of working toward that goal represents progress. Examine every possibility, and don't let rejection slow you down. There is an opportunity out there for you.

*"...Of all people who earn more than $50,000 a year in this country, 65 percent are in sales..."*[1]

# CHAPTER 9 Why not?

I have chosen to devote an entire chapter to the subject of sales. Maybe you believe there is no way in the world you want to make your living in this way. Many high-paid women once felt just like you do. Some of them have used sales as a way to move into other positions, and some have made sales their careers.

My friend Maggie trained a group of women whose company decided to make them salespeople, against their will. When asked why they did not want to do this kind of work, she was told they didn't like salespeople. When she asked why not, she was told salespeople are pushy, obnoxious, fast-talking, and unethical. Hardly the kind of people we want to identify with, or even associate with. She then asked them to describe people who had once helped them make a decision to buy something. Now the response was entirely different. These people were good listeners, helpful, knowledgeable, and empathetic. Somehow, these salespeople were not remembered as salespeople.

Like many professions, sales attracts all kinds of people. Salespeople are more visible than those who do other kinds of jobs, so more opinions are formed about them. In almost any group of salespeople, you can find someone who has at least some of the first traits described. Sometimes we assume that

---

1. Working Women Report p. 48 Barbara Pletcher, founder of the National Association for Professional Saleswomen.

the most aggressive fast-talkers get most of the business. We believe being obnoxious is the price one pays for success. The truth is, the best salespeople (and the richest) have a high level of self-discipline and they are very flexible. Good salespeople adapt their selling style to the buying style of the individual customer at the time.

Perhaps you have nothing against salespeople, but do not believe you have what it takes to do it yourself. While it requires more assertiveness than most female positions, it is certainly nothing that women innately lack.

In spite of how you currently feel about sales, there are several reasons why it might be a good move for you at this point in your career.

- Sales is often seen as a stepping stone to other jobs within your corporation. Many of your executives probably worked in sales at one point.
- Sales is a career that anyone can begin, regardless of age, experience, or education.
- Sales skills are seen as transferable; sales experience in one area can help you land a sales job with another company in another pay range.
- Because sales is so measurable, your value to the corporation can be easily recognized, and is not the subjective evaluation of others. This can be very helpful if you are not interested in learning to play the political games around you.
- Sales is one of the few professions which does not require you to "move up the ladder" or be promoted in order to make more and more money. You never have to become anyone's boss in order to earn a higher income.
- Sales can be more like being self-employed than any other job.

- Sales people and sales managers are among the highest paid people in the country.
- I believe that women bring some unique skills to the job of sales, allowing them to excel. While it is a results-oriented position, it must be performed as a task-oriented job. Many of us take to this very easily. And, if women are in fact more other-oriented, this quality can help us tune into our customers and their needs.

## *On Your Way to Somewhere Else*

In many corporations, outside sales is an entry-level job in a male job track. New people to the organization, or people fresh out of college are hired as salespeople. Previous sales experience may be required, desired, or not expected. Perhaps your goal is a line position in management where you work. You stand a lot better chance of applying for that job as a salesperson than as an administrative person in staff. Find out the background of those people you want to emulate. You might be surprised how many of them served time in the sales force.

Experience in sales helps an executive in several ways. It is crucial for a company to keep a pulse on one's customers and their needs. Most executives need to interact with customers from time to time. Sales is a good training ground for this. Management in every department needs to see things from the customer's viewpoint. *Nothing happens until the sale is made*. Corporations that forget this will be in trouble before long.

## *Room for Everyone*

Yes, anyone can get a job in sales. All kinds of people make good salespeople. There are people of all kinds of personalities who succeed in this profession. People from all kinds of different backgrounds have excelled. Executives know this. Women are succeeding in sales in almost every field. Many women who were stuck in "female" jobs, going nowhere and earning very little are now very wealthy because they learned how to sell.

You may be thinking that you couldn't get a sales job in the corporation you work for. That does not mean you could not get a job in sales. Different companies have different experience levels they require in salespeople. But each of us can find a niche we can fill in this field. That experience can lead us to better and better opportunities within the same company or with another corporation. We will talk later about what to look for when interviewing for a job in sales.

## *Experience Counts*

Because sales experience in one area can transfer to another area, you may accept a position in sales which you do not really want, in order to take that experience elsewhere. Sales experience is almost always seen as more valuable than product or industry knowledge.

Salespeople change jobs more often than other people. There are several reasons for this. Most sales jobs have an earning range, and you will eventually become dissatisfied with one range and want to move on to another. A change in companies may be necessary to do this. Many times the job changes. There is a persistent belief among sales management that doubling the sales force will double sales. If a team of 10 people bring in $2 million worth of business in one year, then 20 people would bring in $4 million next year. If the sales force has territories or assigned accounts, this means that territories are cut in half, while the same level of production is expected. This may be palatable for several years running, but eventually will cause good salespeople to leave for another opportunity. Another way that the job may change is an increase in expectation, or quota. If you are able to bring in $500,000 worth of business this year, then you are sometimes assigned $600,000 as a quota next year. This is another reason why salespeople may move on, leaving the opportunity for someone with less experience who is willing to work for less money.

Your product line may become less competitive, thanks to your competitors or your own management. When this kind of thing happens, and your company loses market share, the salespeople are hit first and hardest. Maybe the company will recover, but a complete turnover in their sales force is a result. Finally, salespeople often get fired. We have said that this is the easiest job in the world to measure. One is measured on sales results, not on effort, and the results are measured within a certain time frame. Salespeople learn to live with this reality. Most good salespeople have been fired at least once.

Because salespeople change companies often, you will find little stigma attached to this practice when you apply for a new sales job. An interviewer told my friend Carol that she had not worked for enough other companies to be considered for that one. Any sales experience you gain anywhere can and will be used to your benefit in looking for another sales opportunity. Remember your expected loyalty to the company. There is nothing unethical or unusual about accepting a position in order to gain experience and move on. Note: sales experience is almost always defined as "outside" sales experience, calling on customers in person. Telemarketing, while a strong skill in itself, is more often downplayed when sales experience is measured. Retail sales experience is also discounted, although there are exceptions.

If you decide you like sales, you can plan your sales career to earn more and more each year until you retire, without ever having to manage others or run a department. You will probably change companies several times, and will have to provide your own retirement income. This is much easier to do when your average income is higher.

Sales is one of the only fields in which you may earn more than your boss, with your boss's blessings. Because your income is usually tied directly to your earnings for the company, your boss and his boss want you to make as much money as possible. Your boss is measured (and usually paid) on the sales results of the team, so your success is important to him. If you currently work for someone who seems to delight in keeping your income low, this will be a refreshing change.

## *Results Count*

Sales by its nature requires you to be self-motivated and disciplined. Because you are measured on your sales results, personality conflicts or differences in work styles are more readily tolerated. In sales, you are on your own more than in most other positions, free to define how to accomplish your goals yourself. If you see your sales job as working for yourself, instead of working for a corporation, you will sell more and earn more.

Salespeople normally have up and down years financially, but earn progressively more over time. Some industries, such as insurance, real estate, or stock brokerages allow one to begin a career, work for the same company (or at least in the same field) throughout her career, earning more and more money until she retires. Salespeople in other industries move from company to company and field to field in order to increase their incomes.

## *A Woman's Place*

Women are selling in almost every field. Some male sales managers have reported to me that, overall, their women outperform their men. One has concluded that the women he hires are smarter than the men he hires. Another has decided that when given the opportunity, they will work hard for a large reward. A third male sales manager told me that women represented 10% of the new salespeople in his corporation. They represented 50% of the *top* new salespeople each year. In other words, the females, while a small proportion of the sales force, were much more likely to become very successful. I believe sales is a results-oriented job, but the process to succeed is very task-oriented. Women with discipline who can learn to close the sale, can make a killing.

## *You Can Learn*

Too many women shy away from lucrative sales jobs because they "don't know anything about" X-Ray equipment, industrial welding, meat-packing software, etc. Most companies find it is easier to teach a salesperson the product than to teach a technician to sell. A salesrep is part of a team of experts, others have the technical knowledge needed. You will be expected to learn on the job, rather than expected to know it all when hired. Typically, the more complicated the product or service, the more money can be made. You will have to grow and learn all of your life. You might as well learn some of the technical information necessary to sell a product line and earn a terrific income. The men interviewing for these jobs are less likely to point out their lack of knowledge, and more likely to stress their ability to learn what is needed.

## *Interviewing*

You may get a job in sales tomorrow. It may or may not be a good opportunity. Much of how we define a good job is how well it pays. People who work on salary don't understand this, but one can interview for a job in sales several times, be offered a position, accept it, and still not know what she will earn.

While most sales positions have no ceiling on potential income earned, there are realistic income ranges that can be expected. Unfortunately, you sometimes will not be quoted this range when you interview. If you are interviewing with the sales manager, he or she may slightly (or greatly) exaggerate the opportunity for which you interview. Don't eliminate a job opportunity just because you think your interviewer is exaggerating. He may be a perfectly good manager otherwise. He isn't exactly lying, there are salespeople working side by side with different income levels, and they never know who will make what amount next year. There may be a new product line coming out which is *expected* to generate new sales. They may have just purchased their major competitor and have all kinds of new customers to call on. They might have recently embarked on an advertising campaign which they *expect* to increase business. Your interviewer is so excited he can hardly contain himself! Each of his people are going to earn at least $100,000 next year. The fact that no salesperson who ever worked there has ever made more than $45,000 does not come up in this conversation. Another sales manager might describe his position more realistically, quoting you a range of $30,000 to $45,000. Try to grab the best opportunity for you, not go to work for the sales manager with the best line. The following are some ways to help you evaluate the job more realistically. We will discuss six considerations.

1. The product or service you will sell.
2. The price range of your product line.
3. Your clientele.
4. Your competition.
5. The company itself.
6. Your compensation.

Your product line is one of the most important. There must be a market for what you sell. This may sound easy to determine, but experts are stumped all the time. Not only must people need or want what you have to offer, but *they* must perceive the need or desire, or you must be able to convince them. If a product has been on the market for awhile, it is easier to determine how strong the market is. However, there is also more competition and many individuals or corporations already have it. A new product or service, or a new twist on the old, might offer great opportunities or great disappointment, or both.

Only a person with no ethics can sell something that she believes is useless or harmful. If the product seems like it would be interesting or exciting to your customers, investigate further. You do *not* have to have personal experience or interest in it. Our own experience usually is limited to those products and services used by consumers. Gale left a job selling industrial controls to one selling industrial plastics. She personally never had use for any of these products. If you limit yourself to selling products that you personally would use, you will eliminate 90% of your opportunities. Certainly don't limit yourself to corporations which you have "heard of." *Do* choose products or services which you think someone else would use and benefit from.

## *How Much?*

Look at the price range of the products you will be selling. Especially if you will be paid mainly with commission, this is a strong consideration. The higher the price, the longer it will take to sell. There are almost no exceptions to this. Don't assume that people who sell products priced at $25,000 earn more money than people selling products priced at $10.00. They may or may not. They earn more money on each sale, but their "sales cycles" are longer. On the other hand, will your customers expect you to drive across town to deliver a $10.00 item? The higher the price, the more will go into the sale, and the fewer customers you will have in any given year. Some salespeople only make two or three sales per year, others make thousands. Try to determine where you would be most comfortable.

## *Customers*

Consider who you will be selling to. Are you selling to individual consumers? If so, in their home? Are you selling to businesses? If so, will you be talking with the chief engineer or the vice president of finance? Will you be selling to individuals who walk into your car dealership? Picture yourself approaching your prospective customers and asking them to buy. Picture yourself explaining the differences between your product and that of your competitors, and using another way to ask them to buy. Some sales jobs require you to develop and maintain a strong relationship with your customers, others require you to make the sale and never see those same people again. Some sales jobs require you to entertain your clients frequently, taking them to dinner, ball games, etc. Other salespeople sell for years without ever taking a customer to lunch.

Ask the interviewer who you are expected to contact and how. "Prospects" are individuals or firms who may possibly buy your product line. If it is a business sale, what size business or what type can use your product or service? "Everyone is a prospect for our product" may simply mean that they have not defined their marketplace. Find out who is most likely to buy, who buys most quickly, who buys the most, according to their experience. Many companies provide you with leads, or lists of people to call on. A *qualified* lead implies that the decision-maker has expressed an interest or readiness to purchase. Any help you can get should be accepted, but don't believe anyone who tells you the prospects are all identified, qualified, and they just need someone to pick up the signed contracts. There are actually sales managers who will say this, some of them believe it. Sales is a hard job. If it weren't, no one would hire salespeople. If it were fairly easy, salespeople wouldn't be paid so well. If it sounds like they don't even need salespeople to do the job, find out more before you make a decision.

## *Opposing Players*

Find out as much as you can about the competitors. If you don't know who they are, ask the person who interviews you. If you get an answer like, "We have no competition," ask what customers are currently doing to handle the problem which this product solves. Ask what kinds of other things people are currently spending their money on. Don't accept "we have no competition," and certainly don't jump at the chance to sell for someone who is so unrealistic. It is wonderful to have a unique product to sell, but all customers have many, many different ways to allocate their budget. Find out how competitors price their products, and how they sell their products. I once interviewed with the president of a software firm. His product cost $45,000 at the time. I asked him how it differed from others I knew of, which cost about $5,000. I was interested in the job, and expected him to have a list of ways in which he blew away the competition. His answer was, "Oh, they're all pretty much the same." Maybe he just didn't know, but I thought the president should know. I didn't pursue the job.

There are some advantages to having the highest quality product, but it will be reflected in your price. There are some advantages to having the lowest price, but it will be reflected in your quality. Too often, we learn all about the competition after we accept the job. Talking to other salespeople will usually tell you more about the competition than talking to management. Don't let competition scare you, but be as knowledgeable as you can before you make a job decision. Typically, the more available business there is perceived to be in a market, the more competition will exist.

## *Company Climate*

Consider the company and people you will be working for. Remember, sales is most like being self-employed, but your immediate boss always makes a difference. Has she ever been in sales? How long ago? You will find it very helpful if your boss understands exactly what you face each day. How well do you think the two of you could get along? I have heard it said that the two most important characteristics of a sales manager are: fairness and organization. Try to get a feel for how fairly she treats the different salespeople and how organized she is. You don't need a sales manager who insists on meeting your top prospect and then doesn't show up for the appointment. If you are new to sales, your sales manager will be more important to you. Will you spend a great deal of time with the sales manager, or will you barely know she exists? Will you need to account for each minute of your day, or is the end result (business brought in) the only thing by which you are measured? Don't expect to have your hand held. The job, by its nature, requires self-discipline and initiative. In this way, it is a lot like running a house. Fortunately, the pay is considerably better.

During the interview process, talk to one or more of the salespeople. Do not ask on the first interview, unless you are offered the job at that time. Once the job is offered, say something like, “I appreciate your offer, and I am very interested in working for you. I would like to talk with a couple of your salespeople about their experiences.” If you meet with resistance, point out that you are entering unknown territory, and would like to know as much as possible about how people have been successful in this job. They will probably be busy. Simply get some names and find out the best time to call them at the office. You can leave your number for them to call you back if they are not in. If the interviewer seems like the type who just wouldn't give you any names, call the office after you leave and ask for a sales representative.

Try to talk to some experienced people. Begin the conversation by explaining that you have been offered a position in their company and are interested in accepting. Ask them how they like the job, the conditions, and the personnel. Ask them about the competition, their strategies, and pricing schedule as compared to their own. If you have been given a quota, tell the other salespeople what it is and ask if they think it is realistic. While it is common for different salespeople to have different quotas, it is also common for them to discuss them between themselves. If there is no quota, ask what level of production you could expect to obtain in your first year. You will probably find them very helpful and cooperative. If not, just talk to someone else. Sales is a competitive field, and they may see anyone new as a threat. They may be sensitive about giving up some of their territory to anyone, even you.

## *Compensation*

There are infinite ways to pay a sales force. If you are paid on straight commission you will not earn anything unless you sell something. Some commission salespeople are responsible for paying their own taxes and social security, and deducting their own expenses from their commission. Some corporations provide their employees with benefits and expenses, and pay straight commission on sales. Straight commission, by its natures, scares women, by their upbringing. The highest paid and the lowest paid salespeople work on straight commission. Too often, women refuse to consider jobs which pay this way, eliminating opportunities to make a good living and/or develop their careers. This is true even when they have other means of support at the time.

If the pay is straight commission, find out if you are to be paid when you bring in an order, or when the customer pays. If you are paid when the company is paid, and your delivery schedule is six weeks long and your terms are net 30 days, you will not be paid for 2 1/2 months after the sale. You will need to consider this when you take the job. You may need to have a means of support for a few months (or longer) until you get rolling.

Another way to pay salespeople is straight salary. This sounds attractive to many people who are not used to sales or who are used to a salary. Typically, companies who pay straight salary want their salespeople to spend a lot of their time building and maintaining relationships with customers, rather than making a sale and moving on to the next prospect. Another reason for this type of pay is that it is an "indirect sale." You might, for instance, educate doctors and pharmacists on your product line and encourage prescriptions. The third reason to pay salespeople straight salary is that it is perceived as cheaper for the corporation. There is nothing wrong with straight salary, but if you are looking for a career in sales, do not limit yourself to jobs which pay this way. If you are considering one, find out what kind of financial rewards accompany high performance. Remember, sales results (not effort) are one of the easiest of all things to measure. If you are very successful, what is the result? Bonuses? Pay increase? Pat on the back? Job security?

Actually, most sales jobs fall somewhere between straight commission and straight salary. A "draw against commission" is a loan which the company makes to you against future commission you will earn. Again, many women do not like to work on a draw because they "owe" the company money. However, there are some real advantages to this type of pay. You have the assurance that the company is investing in you, even if you are not producing. You have use of the money sooner, always an advantage financially. Most importantly, a draw helps to even out your income so it can be more predictable and you can more easily pay your bills. If you are offered a straight commission job, you can sometimes negotiate for a draw. If you are offered a draw, take it.

Salary plus commission is common. Generally speaking, the more "salary-based" (percentage of total income from salary) that is paid, the more extra-curricular activities will be required. You may be required to attend more meetings, train new people, or help design promotional literature. These things may be an interesting change of pace, but will detract from your sales effort.

There are as many ways of paying salespeople as there are companies in this country. I sold for a large corporation who's formula was so complex that is took salespeople several hours each month to find out if our paychecks were correct. Sometimes a job is more salary-based when one begins, and becomes more commission-based through time. This is a good indication that the company is willing to take more of the risk up-front to get good people, and willing to pay them what they earn when they are experienced, to help keep them around.

## *Traveling?*

Many people assume that a job in sales translates into a job on the road. Some of them do, but many other jobs do not. Many sales jobs require you to be out of town a couple of times a year for some reason, but this is the extent of traveling. While one sales rep might have a three-state territory, another rep (not usually in the same industry) will have a territory of three city blocks. If you are interested in a sales career, decide how much travel you would like to do before you begin to interview. This will give you a basis from which to compare your opportunities. You may take a job which requires more travel than you would like, just because you want the job. You may enjoy traveling more or less than you expected. Remember your new definition of loyalty.

Don't turn down a job which requires travel because you plan to have a baby three years from now. My friend Alice traveled 3 or 4 nights a week before she had her son. When he was about 8 months old, she decided it was not worth it. Her experience allowed her to get a job selling for a major corporation, in town, 3 days per week. Without that sales experience, she could not have landed the part-time position which suited her later.

## *Other Considerations*

If you cannot find a job in outside sales, a telemarketing job is a good training ground, and can be a very fun job. Remember, however, that it is not perceived as real sales experience, and it usually does not pay nearly as well, so continue to search for an outside job. It is my personal opinion that someone who can sell well on the telephone can sell anything, but this is not the perception in the marketplace. Almost without exception, you are better to have outside sales experience than telemarketing experience when you move to your next job.

Some companies use their telephone sales and service desk as a training ground for outside sales. If you interview for such a position, consider it *seriously*. It can provide you with a great knowledge of the product line and contact with customers before you go out on the street. It is also a good opportunity to learn to use the telephone effectively, a real asset in any sales job. Try to pin your interviewer down as to how long it will be before you are promoted, and don't forget that is your goal.

So, now you know some of the reasons why you should consider sales and what to look for in a sales job. If you decide on a position in sales, you will want to learn more about the process of selling. Visit your local bookstore and library, there are many excellent books to help you learn how to sell and earn a great living. Professional salespeople hold seminars and training regularly. Some are well worth attending.

Yes, it is a roller coaster career in many ways. You are on the front line, your income fluctuates wildly, and you probably change jobs frequently. Millions of highly-paid men and women cannot imagine making their living any other way.

## Computer Sales Opportunity

Computer System and Peripheral company is in need of several Inside Sales/Customer Service personnel. Job responsibilities include customer and company sales contacts. Above average income can be expected from these positions. Computer and Sales experience desired, but may not be mandatory.

Inc. offers a competitive salary with a full range of benefits. Qualified candidates should send resume including salary history to:

## AUTOMOBILE SALESPERSON

mazda SUBARU

**MOTORS INC.** has expanded! We now carry the full Subaru line as well as Mazda. We need you to help with the extra new car traffic. Experience is a plus. Enthusiasm is required. Call or stop by for more info.

## GRAPHIC SALES REP

Established growing graphics company needs a professional, self-starter to sell color, mounting, laminating, and copy services to the business community. Good communication skills and strong work ethic required. Past experience helpful, but not required. Protected territory. Salary plus commission limited only by your efforts. For a confidential interview call Cheryl at

SALES REPRESENTATIVE
Construction & Mining Industry

Major manufacturer seeks self motivated individual to call on distributors & end users in well established territory. Position is based in & requires extensive travel in midwest. Degree preferred, experienced or entry level. Compensation based on experience. Send resume w/salary history to:

---

ADVERTISING/SALES
Bright, Outgoing.
Warm, Friendly,
Sense of Humor!

If these describe you, please apply to **name removed**, a 35 yr. old national women-oriented advertising co. Fund-raising, sales exp. a plus. Flexible day hours, excellent benefits 401(k). $30-60. Bonuses. Incentives. Car req'd. Auto reimbursement.

---

## INDUSTRIAL SALES

H , a leader in the material handling industry, has a great opportunity for someone trying to get a start in sales. We are looking for a self-driven, energetic person to take over one of our central Ohio territories. Looking especially for recent college graduates in search of a career in sales. If intrigued, please call

---

## CAREER OPPORTUNITY IN FINANCIAL SERVICES

M L is looking for people with entrepreneurial skills and a driving ambition. Qualified trainees can earn up to $800 per week in our paid Career Skills Training program, which enables you to learn what you need to know to succeed in sales while you earn level initial compensation. Once appointed as an Account Representative, you'll be supported by a state-of-the-art computerized marketing system, receive an attractive benefits package, and quarterly incentive opportunities.

*"Like any effective piece of advertising, your resume must have good form and content. It should look and read like good advertising copy – grab attention and motivate the reader to take action."*[1]

CHAPTER 10

# Write a Resume

An excellent resume is a crucial part of your job search. Your resume speaks for you to potential employers, who don't know you and who compare it with the many, many other resumes they receive. Perfecting your resume should be an ongoing process.

Your resume needs to sell your potential, making you stand out in a crowd. ***Its purpose is to get you interviews.*** Its very writing can help you define your strengths, gain confidence, and determine your career objectives. As you spread the word that you are in the market for a new position, you will also want to get your resume into circulation.

Donald Asher, author of *The Overnight Resume*, believes a resume is equally important before and after the interview. Once the interview is over, the resume reminds the interviewer of what you have to offer. If your resume is written well, you are more likely to be remembered as articulate and intelligent.

---

1. Krannich, Ronald, & Banis, William. (1988). *High Impact Resumes & Letters* (p. 38). Manassas, VA: Impact Publications.

Knowing the importance of a resume, both before and after the interview, need not intimidate you. Everyone finds resume writing difficult. The worst thing you can do is postpone the task.

## *Give It a Professional Look*

If you have a computer or word processor at home, write it there. If you do not have a good-quality printer, take the resume file on a disk to a local printer to have it printed. If you have a computer where you work, stay after hours and work on your resume if possible. If these are not options, try to borrow someone else's computer or word processor for this task. Your resume will change as you clarify your objectives and interview. For this reason, make sure it is easy for you to make changes. However, don't wait until your resume is completely, absolutely perfect to send it out.

This is not the time to be cute. Use black ink. The only acceptable colors for paper are white and slightly off-white. Use standard 8-1/2 x 11 letter-size paper. If you use other sizes, your resume could be thrown away just because it is too large or small to fit with the others. Have your resume printed or copied on heavy paper; it will only cost a little more and will make a better impression. Send it in an envelope that is large enough so that you don't need to fold the resume. Be sure to apply adequate postage.

There is some debate as to the ideal length of a resume, but one page is always acceptable. More than two pages is unacceptable. Typically, your resume will get about 15 seconds of someone's attention, so don't waste your words. What you say is important, but the layout must be visually appealing, too. This is not a novel the reader will curl up with. Most readers will skim your resume, so make it easy to skim. By definition, your resume is a synopsis of your credentials. You want the reader to decide within 15 seconds to ask you in for an interview. That's all you're working for.

In the rest of this chapter I will touch on a few highlights of various resume formats, as well as offer a few tips for writing your resume. This vast subject is beyond the scope of this book. I recommend that you consult the many excellent books available on the topic at your library or local bookstore.

## *Identify Yourself*

Whatever your format, your name, address, and phone number (including area code) should be at the top of your resume, either centered or left-justified at the left margin. Use your home phone number, since most interviewers will not want to call you at your current place of employment. Use your full name. Do not use any titles such as Ms. or Mrs., unless Dr. is appropriate. Do not include a picture, unless you are trying to land a job as a model. Do not provide any information about age, height, weight, marital status, religion, or sexual preference.

Make sure that anyone living with you – roommates, children, or anyone else – can answer the telephone and carefully take a message. If needed, instruct them on how to do so. If you do not have an answering machine at home, now is the time to get one, or sign up for voice mail. Someone may try to get in touch with you only once, and then go on to the next resume. No one will hold it against you if you are not at home 24 hours a day, but not having an answering machine could work against you. Alternative phone numbers, such as your mother's, are not acceptable. Don't ask a busy employer to dial two different numbers trying to reach you.

## *Your Career Objective*

The next thing on your resume should be your career objective, even though you may write it later. This item is missing from many resumes, but it should not be missing from yours. You want to be considered for new and different opportunities. It is tough to come up with, and it will change with different interview opportunities, but it says more about you than much of the rest of the resume. With only 15 seconds for reading, you need the impact of this career objective.

The career objective should be one sentence describing what you want and what you have to offer. Krannich and Banis, authors of *High Impact Resumes & Letters*, emphasize that the career objective should be work-centered, not self-centered. It should not describe what you want the company to do for you.

I have told you to keep your options open and consider any and all opportunities. Now I'm asking you to come up with a specific career objective and write it down for the world to see. You must constantly project the image of someone who knows what she wants and is working toward it, even if you're not as sure as you act. There is nothing wrong or dishonest about looking in several career directions at any given time. As opportunities arise that look interesting, you will want to write appropriate career objectives. Once you land a good job in the right career lane, other options will fade from your mind. You have a lot to offer many different kinds of employers. Let them each know it.

A weak, self-centered objective might be:

> *A copywriter position with opportunity for rapid advancement.*

Maybe that is what you are after, but this objective gives the employer no incentive to hire you over someone else.

A strong, work-centered objective might be:

> *A chance to increase sales by helping buyers make the right choice. An opportunity to utilize strong communication skills and creative ideas.*

If you are still convinced that you lack "qualifications," think about the skills that you have and how you might best present these skills in your career objective. This is good practice for interviewing, where you will need to stress the skills you can transfer to a new position. It is time for women to concentrate on transferable skills, instead of our lack of experience. The shift in emphasis can help us appear and eventually become more confident, less intimidated, and thus more qualified to do the job.

Remember, companies generally expect to train someone on the job. They rarely expect someone to slide in and perform perfectly and single-handedly the first day on the job.

## *What You Have to Offer*

After the objective comes the body of the resume. There are several formats for the body, and you may end up with several versions of your resume with various formats. Whatever format you choose, your purpose is the same.

Be sure to define your abilities, not your past or present duties. This is where many women slip up. We are often so task-oriented that we want to describe our duties in great detail, sure that anyone will be impressed with our capacity to get a lot done. Forget it. You are ready to break new ground, not find another job just like the one you have. It is tougher to write about your abilities, but the effect is much more powerful.

Too many of us spend our entire resume on what we have done. When we do this, we are asking to be considered only for work similar to what we have done before. We promise nothing else. We leave it up to the reader to interpret what our strengths are and what we are able to do for the company. To some employers, how you present yourself in the resume may indicate how you will present yourself in an interview and how you will perform the job. Your resume should somehow naturally address your pattern of strengths and what you are likely to contribute to your future employer.

At this point it may be helpful to do some soul-searching to help you determine what you want and what you do well. Think about your achievements throughout life. What have you accomplished, both personally and professionally? Especially think about things that seemed impossible at the time. Maybe you saw your way out of a painful marriage, or perhaps you wrote a difficult report. Don't think about all your failures and why they happened. Job searching is not the time to reduce your confidence level. Listing and thinking through your accomplishments can help you apply your skills to the jobs you seek. Think about those things you do well, but try not to be too specific. You may well end up doing something you currently don't know exists. If you are good at convincing others to see things your way, or good at concentrating on a project until its completion, or good at doing several things at once, these are things to note about yourself. Don't assume you have less than others to offer potential employers.

Too often we think of skills in narrow terms of technical skills or skills that have a highly specific range of application. When we define our skills in this way, we severely limit what we are willing to offer potential employers. As I have pointed out, most skills, and usually the most important ones, can be transferred from one career to another. Are you good at communicating? Can you motivate? Observe? Plan? Conduct research? Delegate? Initiate? Are you conscientious? Energetic? Positive? Reliable?

You have more than your share of skills. Some are worth noting on your resume. If you have something great to say about yourself, don't save it for the interview. You won't get the opportunity if your resume is not sufficiently impressive.

## *Quantify Your Value*

Any time you can provide your reader with facts or figures on your resume, do so. Nothing can be more impressive or easier to interpret. All employers are looking for people who demonstrate a bottom-line orientation, who are concerned about increasing revenue and decreasing costs. You have probably been involved in such efforts in the past, even if you didn't invent them. Dig up the facts and present them on your resume.

Even if you can only quantify one accomplishment, such as, "Department reduced late payments by 32%," be sure to include it. Not only can the employer better evaluate your success, you appear to be a results-oriented person, and we all know what that means.

Many of us find it hard to see our experience as significant, our achievements as worth noting. Don't be discouraged or intimidated by the seemingly high-powered experience of others. They are just people doing their jobs. To see ourselves and our efforts as unimportant will cause us to come across as unimportant, even on paper. We have much to offer. We may have a lot to learn, but we are quite capable of learning. Sometimes we grow the most from what might seem to be insignificant experience. Project your strengths. Don't lie about your background, but don't underestimate yourself.

Hard working instruction-takers need not apply. Describe yourself and your experiences in terms of the responsibility you can shoulder, not the effort you put in. Make every sentence and statement reflect the employer's needs and what will be gained by hiring you. Most other applicants won't write this way.

## *Formats*

The most common resume format uses a reverse chronological order. Starting with your most recent employment, the resume lists your work experience backwards by date. There is nothing wrong with this type of resume. It is like most others the employer will see, but it may not be right for you. Since it tends to focus on positions held, rather than skills, it may be ineffective for those wishing to change career paths.

A second format is the functional format, which concentrates on your qualifications and skills. It says very little about positions and dates.

A third type is a combination of the two, which includes a section on the history of your employment, but brings out the strengths you want to stress.

Whatever your format, concentrate on accomplishments and potential, rather than duties. Put everything in terms of the advantage to the employer in hiring you.

## *Just Get Started*

Start writing. Later your rewriting will help perfect the resume. Just get started by writing as much as you can think of. Style, format, and specific phrases can come later. Think of your skills, and make note of them. Later, you can think of how they might apply to individual jobs. Your phrasing will become more and more important as your resume gets closer to being done. Sometimes substituting one word for another will make a sentence, and the resume, more powerful. In the meantime, just start writing. The first few drafts of your resume will probably be longer than one page, but don't worry about length at this time. At some point you will feel ready to make it read as a resume should.

Some people provide names and addresses of references on their resume, but I don't recommend using the space for this. You can put "References on Request" if you want to, but even that is not necessary. An employer who wants to request a reference will do so whether you state it on your resume or not.

There is more to be said about writing a resume. Get started on yours, and refer to publications that are dedicated to the subject. Give it to a savvy friend to review. Give it to another friend to review. Rewrite, rewrite, and rewrite, even if you are passing it out in the meantime. Ask your interviewers what they think of your resume and what you could do to improve it.

## *The Cover Letter*

Employers receive many resumes, especially after they advertise a position. After spending so much time and energy on your resume, you don't want to let it get lost in the shuffle. An excellent cover letter is the best way to help you stand out as a candidate and get someone to read your resume.

Here I go again – giving you something else to compose and perfect. Cover letters can be painful to write, but you only need one job. This letter to this next employer could lead to the job for you.

Address the cover letter to an individual, not a company. Try to avoid the human resources department if possible. If an ad in the newspaper gives a name, then address your cover letter to that person, unless you have a better contact at the company.

Before you send any correspondence, it is always best to call and make sure of the correct spelling of the person's name and title. You might have found the Vice President of Sales listed in the Chamber of Commerce directory as Mr. Kevin Moore. Before you write him, call. Simply tell the person answering the phone that you have something to send to Kevin Moore and you would like to verify his name and title. It may be that Kevin Moore is now president, and a new vice president has taken his place, or his name is spelled More, or his first name is Keith, or he is Dr. Moore, or his title is Division Manager. Also verify the exact name and spelling of the company. You will be surprised at how often you had it wrong. You will be far ahead of the game if you simply make one phone call before sending any correspondence.

Simply sending a cover letter with your resume will help you stand out, because many people do not. When you send a good cover letter, you will dramatically increase your chances of an interview. Again, time restrictions may force you to send a resume without a cover letter or to send a cover letter that is less than ideal. Timing is almost always more important than perfection. Have some cover letters ready on a computer or word processor. You will need to make some changes for each one you send, but having a basic layout and most of the writing done will help save time

Your cover letter should be specific to the job or the advertisement. It should be a letter that could be written only by you, no one else. See if it passes both these tests before sending it out.

## *Follow-Up*

Don't assume your resume will get to where you intended after you mail it. It's a good idea to follow up in a few days with a phone call to make sure the employer received your letter and resume.

Resumes are hard to construct, but everyone sees them that way. All the resumes that compete against yours were written by people who also found them difficult to prepare. Exciting jobs have been forfeited and hundreds of thousands of dollars lost because qualified people didn't bother to prepare a resume or write a good one. Get started on your resume right away. Writing means rewriting over and over, so keep working on it, even as you interview.

*"Sometimes there is only a hairline's difference among candidates. When that is the case, it's the neatest hairline that wins."*[1]

CHAPTER 11

# How to Interview

The job is secured or lost in the interview. All the credentials in the world cannot replace the impression you make on the interviewer. People operate businesses, and people have to work with people. How you listen, speak, sit, stand, react, question, smile and laugh in the interview all help determine whether or not you get the job.

Far too many of us are unprepared when we interview. It may be that we squeeze interviews in between other obligations. We may already be convinced that we can't get the job or don't want it.

Try to approach every interview as if it were the only thing you have to do that day. Do your very best, even if there is no way in the world you want the job. The interview is a time when your new found confidence can really make a difference. To increase your confidence in interviewing, practice and be prepared.

As tight as your schedule may be, try to schedule as many interviews as possible. Some of these will be practice interviews.

---

1. Martin, Phyllis. (1987). *Martin's Magic Formula for Getting the Right Job* (p. 5). New York: St. Martin's Press.

It may be tough to get away from work for a job interview, but employers understand this. Many will interview you before working hours, on a lunch hour, or in the evening after work. Always interview as if you were interested in the position. Many people have accepted jobs that began with practice interviews.

## *Look Your Best, No Excuses*

We have discussed appearance at length and now is the time to implement all you know. So what if you are dressed more professionally than the interviewer? That person already has a job. If you have only one dark business suit, wear the same suit to every interview. When you go back for a second interview, wear a different blouse.

Martin tells us that some employers think they can learn about an applicant's energy by the way she sits or walks. Watch your posture.

Look your professional best, and project confidence. You may be convinced that this employment decision will come down to who is the most "qualified" or "experienced" person. Time and again, the most experienced people are not hired, not because they lack expertise, but because they lack something else the interviewer was looking for. We learn much of the specific knowledge we need on a job after we are hired. Interviewers know this. Relax, establish a rapport with the interviewer, and sell yourself.

## *The Employment Application*

Part of the interview process may be an employment application. If you are not asked to complete an application, don't bring it up. Many employers have them, but don't always use them. If you have the opportunity to take the application home and complete it, do so. That will give you a chance to complete it accurately and legibly. You should type it if possible. It will also give you an excuse to come back to the employer, since you will have to return the completed form. In case you do have to fill out an application there, be prepared. Have a pen and all the necessary facts, such as your previous employers' addresses, and the names, addresses, and phone numbers of your references.

Although it is against the law, some application forms ask questions that are not pertinent to the job at hand. Women especially need to be aware of these questions because they can be used against us. It has been said that the best job candidates are married men or single women, and many people still hold to this. Do not answer questions about your marital status, number of children, age, race, religion, height, or weight. Anybody who puts these questions on an employment application may want to use the information to make employment decisions, and that amounts to discrimination. They will need much of this information once you are hired, but that is a different issue. Don't let them use such information to make a hiring decision.

Try also to avoid giving your current salary. It's better not to give them a figure to start with, even before they interview you. If they insist, think about adding 35-40% to your salary to include the value of your benefits, if you receive any.

## *The Aptitude Test*

Welcome any and all tests administered to you. You will probably not be asked to take one unless you are a serious candidate, so it may be a good sign. Many people have moved from one line of work into another because tests showed they were capable, making prior direct experience unnecessary. Relax and do your best on the test. Think of it as a great opportunity to demonstrate your strengths.

## *Once You're in the Door*

There are a few rules to follow every time. Always introduce yourself, pronouncing your name clearly and slowly. Shake the interviewer's hand, whether it is a man or woman. Do not wait for the interviewer to extend a hand, but reach out first to shake hands. Of course, shake firmly. As you shake hands, look the interviewer in the eye, smile, and repeat the person's name. This will help you remember it. Do not chew gum. Do not smoke, even if the interviewer smokes. Do not eat. All you need is the cream from a donut falling in the middle of your lap to distract you from the interviewing process. If the atmosphere is friendly and relaxed, accept a cup of coffee if it is offered and you want it. Keep in mind that you might spill it, or you might find it difficult to find a place to set your cup. If the interview is long, additional liquid might cause you to ask for a break to use the rest room at an inappropriate time. If you are taken to lunch as part of the interview, eat then, of course, but do not drink alcohol. It may affect your speech or thought process. If someone won't hire you because you won't have a drink in the middle of the day, you don't want to work for that person anyway.

Once the introductions and handshakes are over, the interview can begin. Things usually start off with small talk about the weather, traffic, and so on. If you have read something interesting about the company, ask about it now. Remember this is a human being you're dealing with, not a god or a monster. Both of you will be happier and the interview will go much better if you can establish a rapport of equals, maybe even friends. Many a hiring decision has been made, not for qualifications and background, but for rapport. As we have said, people have to work with people, and all the experience in the world cannot make up for lack of chemistry between two people. I am *not* talking about sexual chemistry, of course. Don't even think of flirting during an interview.

The issue of rapport is important even if you will not be working for the interviewer directly. I once developed an easy rapport with the interviewer in a large corporation. I was hired and worked there several years. I never saw that man after the interview, but I know it was he who made the hiring decision. I believe it was our rapport, more than my qualifications, that landed me the job. Make eye contact, but don't stare into the interviewer's eyes. Even if you are physically cold, don't fold your arms across your chest. I have known employers who won't hire people who fold their arms. Leaning back in your chair is a sign of relaxing. Sitting forward in your chair is a sign of interest or enthusiasm. Don't be rigid during an interview. Change your position, but don't slouch. Stand up and move around if the occasion permits.

Project confidence. Getting into a panic over whether we will get the job causes many of us to lose confidence. Projecting a lack of confidence can cause us to bomb the interview. This is where practice interviews can help us. The more interviews you have had, the easier it will be to project confidence. No matter how much you think you want the job, keep this in mind. You do not have this job now. If you don't get the job, you will be right where you are now. You will have lost nothing. It is okay to want the job, but it is not okay to panic over it. A strategy I have used is to pretend in my mind that I do not want the position. This helps me relax and project confidence.

If more than one other person is in the room, try not to be intimidated. Greet them all with a smile, because this is a very good sign. No company allocates several people's time unless it is close to a hiring decision. Be sure to look around the room and address everyone as you speak, even if only one person is questioning you. You will probably not know the dynamics of this decision or who has the most influence. This may sound like a lot of things to remember. If you can relax and have confidence, all this will be easier and more natural.

## *You Interview Them*

You are here for two reasons. You need to find out about the company and the job, and the interviewer needs to find out about you. Your job in the interview is to discover as much as you can about the position in question. The interviewer's job is to find out about you. Too often we plan our strategy to complete the interviewer's objective, but not our own.

You would not have gotten to the interview if you were not being considered for the job. They may have already decided to hire you, based on your resume or previous interviews. Try to assume this is the case. You will be less nervous and more intent on finding out more about the company.

Question the interviewer. This approach serves several purposes. It directs the line of questioning away from you for a while, helps you determine if you are in fact interested in the position, and adds some value to your services. You are a valuable commodity. You cannot afford to work just anywhere. If you demonstrate that you are selective in your employment choices, you will be perceived as much more valuable.

If the interviewer has a lot to say, great. I have found that the more talking the interviewer does, the more likely I am to get a job offer. This makes sense, since people are not as impressed with what we say to them as with what they say to us. Keep asking questions about the job to keep the interviewer talking. Of course, show interest in what is being said.

If the interviewer will not talk, don't be intimidated. The interviewer may be trying to intimidate you, may be testing you, or may simply be hard to talk with. Don't worry about whether or not the interviewer is playing mind games with you. The less the interviewer talks, the more specific your questions should be. Instead of saying, "Tell me about this job," say something like, "Will I report directly to you?" Or say, "So, then, my primary responsibility in this job will be to keep existing customers happy by addressing their immediate concerns. Is that right?" Even if you just get short answers, you are extracting information, and you are more in control of the interview.

## *They Interview You*

If this part can go smoothly, you will have more energy and presence of mind to question the employer about the job. Relax, smile, laugh as much as possible, and knock 'em dead.

If the conversation never gets around to you and your background, the hiring decision might have been made already. Don't talk yourself out of an offer. Occasionally, a hiring decision is made without your having to say much. If the interviewer says something like, "Any more questions?" you can ask, "Do you believe I am right for this position?" or "Do you have any hesitations about hiring me?" or "What do you think of hiring me for this job?" You may get the offer on the spot. You may find out exactly what they are looking for, and you can adapt your responses accordingly.

Usually, the interviewer will spend some time asking you questions and listening to your responses. The larger the company, the more formal this process may be. After reading this chapter, try to formulate some responses in your mind. Listen very carefully to what is asked and said. Giving a perfect answer to the wrong question can cost you a job.

## *None of Their Business*

In addition to inappropriate questions on an application, some interviewers routinely ask illegal questions of applicants during the interview. Many are unaware of the current laws, and others don't care. Answers to these illegal questions can cost you an opportunity. People make assumptions based on this information. These assumptions may or may not be accurate. If you are single, it may be assumed that you are more dedicated to your career *or* that your social life will interfere with the job. If you are married, it may be assumed that your husband's career takes precedence over yours *or* that you are more settled down and steady. If you have no children, it may be assumed that you want to dedicate your energies to your work *or* that you will have children any time now and they would have to replace you. If you are a single parent, it may be assumed that you will be more dedicated because you need the job *or* that parental obligations will interfere with your work effort. These assumptions will most likely be based on the personal bias of the interviewer and not on the hiring experience of the corporation. Whatever the source, these assumptions are beyond your control, so keep this kind of information as limited as possible.

Another reason to avoid disclosing too much personal information is that it may lead to more and more inappropriate questioning. You may be asked how your husband would feel about your making more money than he does. You might be asked how your husband would feel about your taking business trips with other men. When this happens, the line of questioning has clearly taken a wrong turn. It is that much harder to get back to the subject of whether you are qualified to do the job.

While many interviewers ask these kinds of questions, I believe they are much more likely to do so if the applicant is wearing a wedding or engagement ring. Wearing a ring is sometimes seen as permission to ask you whatever personal questions they want. Leave your rings at home.

Your goal should be to get out of this line of questioning and back to the interview as quickly as you can gracefully do it. A friendly comment, "I guess I don't see how my marital status is relevant to the requirements of the position," may accomplish it. Be sure to be quiet and give the interviewer a chance to respond. Don't barrel forward like you have something to hide.

Don't accuse the interviewer of breaking the law; but another approach is to act surprised and say something like, "Gosh, I'm surprised you are required to ask that question, given the laws against it." Again, wait for the interviewer to respond.

Consider what the interviewer is trying to find out. Does this person really care if you have children or not? The interviewer is concerned about your commitment to the job and to the company. This person goes by the same rules we have discussed earlier, fierce loyalty for today, but this value is not communicated in the interview. No company is anxious to train employees and then lose them for any reason. Every interviewer knows that people leave companies all the time. When asked if you plan to have children, try this answer: "Are you concerned that my family obligations would interfere with my job performance?" The subject might be dropped, or you might be told that the company is concerned you will leave the job if you have children. "I can assure you that my commitment to the job at hand is as strong as anyone you will interview." Your goal is not to disclose the details of your private life, but to get the interview back on track.

## *What's Different?*

A results-oriented position requires more initiative, drive, assertiveness, and risk than a task-oriented position. For this reason, the interviewing process will usually be a little different.

Women are sometimes hesitant to discuss their accomplishments and achievements, afraid they might sound boastful. Try to remember that you are competing for this job with other people. Your competition is bragging about themselves. They are highlighting their strengths, so you need to highlight yours. Modesty at this point may make you appear less capable than other applicants. You cannot expect the interviewer to interpret what you say and determine what you mean. If you have done well in a certain area, say so. Women typically have not pointed out our own strengths and are therefore often seen as not fully participating or contributing. Showing some boldness in the interview may help you gain respect. You know yourself. There are shy women and outspoken women and every kind in between. Just because you are shy does not mean you always have to act shy. You can learn to express yourself, and there is no better time than now.

You may be asked open-ended questions, such as, "Why do you want this job? Why do you think you can do this job?" If the interviewer has offered no explanation of the job, and you only know what was printed in the newspaper ad, don't jump in with both feet to explain why you want it. Say something like, "I believe I am interested in this position, but I need to know a little more about it before I can say whether it is a good fit. What exactly is the function of this position in your organization? How does this position contribute to the profit of this department? What are the goals of someone in this job, and what time frame is used to measure success? How are the results measured? What is the career path of someone who starts in this position?" Any or all of these questions might be appropriate. Try to stay away from discussions of all the tasks normally completed to execute the job, or you may appear too task-oriented.

## *Concentrate on Your Potential*

Too often we want to be able to move right into a job and do it tomorrow – single-handedly, of course. Remember, the average man figures he is qualified if he has 40 percent of the skills needed on any given job. You need to see yourself as qualified, even if you have never done many of the things involved. If you are moving from a female to a male job, you probably won't have done this type of job before, but don't disqualify yourself. No matter who they hire, the person will not have done precisely the same job elsewhere. They might actually be looking for someone who has no experience in this exact area, for a fresh approach to the job. Relax, concentrate on your potential instead of your experience, and try to encourage the interviewer to talk.

## *Questions and Answers*

Phyllis Martin[2] provides a detailed list of questions you may be asked in an interview. I have listed these on the following pages, and I offer suggestions for answering each question.

My suggestions assume you work in a female-dominated profession and you are now interviewing for a position in a male-dominated career path. As Martin advises, remember to answer the interviewer's question, not another one. Don't volunteer a lot of information that is not asked, especially if it does not put you in a favorable light. The goal is not to be dishonest, but to be prepared.

For most of these questions, thoughtful planning can prepare you for any interview, no matter what the position. Think about how you might answer each question. Try to clarify your own preferences and consider how to present your opinions in the most favorable light. Prepare to ask questions of your own.

---

2. Copyright © 1987 by Phyllis Martin
From MARTIN'S MAGIC FORMULA FOR GETTING THE RIGHT JOB
By Phyllis Martin Reprinted by permission of St. Martin's Press Incorporated

### Martin's Interviewing Questions[a]

| Martin's Questions | My Suggestions for Answering the Questions |
|---|---|
| **1. What do you know about us?** | Nothing pegs you as an amateur faster than having no idea what the company does or sells. Before the interview, go to the library and read about the company. Ask the business reference librarian for help. You can quickly learn a lot about what the company does, as well as more about its financial performance than many of its employees know. Get on the Internet and search for information about the company. You don't need to know everything, but learn what you can. |
| **2. What can you tell me about your current job?** | Talk about your job in terms of the challenges you face and the responsibilities you hold. Include any result-oriented activities that you perform. If you manage people, even one other person, mention this first. Don't describe a typical day and the tasks you perform, unless you are asked. Speak of the results you produce, the goals you accomplish, and the team you are a part of: "Our goal is to speed up the process of billing and collecting, to get the most use of money received. We bill each customer on receipt of product and collect payables in the most timely manner possible. In this way, we maximize cash flow." |

Martin's Interviewing Questions[a] (Continued)

| Martin's Questions | My Suggestions for Answering the Questions |
| --- | --- |
| **3. What do you think determines a person's progress in a good company?** | Do not give the good-little-girl answer, "Whoever does the job well will be recognized and promoted." Try instead, "I believe a good company should recognize employees who produce results that meet or exceed goals. The company should promote those who demonstrate leadership by identifying and solving problems with innovative methods." |
| **4. Are you looking for a permanent or a temporary job?** | As long as you are planning to work for at least six months, say you want a permanent job. If the job is temporary but you suspect it could lead to permanent employment, or if you think it will look good on your resume, you might respond, "I am looking for permanent employment, but I believe this temporary position you offer will be a good career move for me." Do not bring up personal reasons for your preference. |

Martin's Interviewing Questions[a] (Continued)

| Martin's Questions | My Suggestions for Answering the Questions |
|---|---|
| **5. Do you prefer to work with others, or do you prefer to work alone? Why?** | Most results-oriented positions require both skills, and most of us need both to function well. You will probably want to say that you prefer a combination of both and then explain. Working alone allows you to become absorbed in your work and concentrate on the end result. Use terms like *self-disciplined* or *self-motivated* when discussing the advantages of working alone. Don't talk about working at your own pace, which may leave the impression that you work slowly. Working with others allows you to combine the experience and efforts of several people to accomplish a common goal. Try to use the word *team* in your response. Don't discuss how well you get along with others; the company is not looking for a social butterfly. Of course, if you know that the job requires you to work completely alone 95% of the time, concentrate more on why you work well alone. Remember, however, that this job may be a stepping stone. If you are promoted, you may never work alone again. Don't close the door on yourself. |

Martin's Interviewing Questions[a] (Continued)

| Martin's Questions | My Suggestions for Answering the Questions |
|---|---|
| **6. What percentage of your educational expenses did you earn? How?** | The more you shouldered yourself, the better. Try to put it in specific terms, "I paid 100% of my college expenses, some of which I paid after I graduated," or "I worked as a salesclerk in a department store about 15 hours a week and paid for as much as I could." If you did not go to college, talk about any outside work you did while in high school: baby-sitting, delivering papers, mowing grass, anything. Some of the highest-paid people in this country have done the most menial jobs. Never be ashamed of honest work you have done. |
| **7. If you had a choice of any job, anywhere, what would you choose to do?** | Don't say that the job you're interviewing for is your absolute, ultimate choice because the interviewer won't believe you. A good answer would be a job that this position could lead to. For instance, if you are interviewing for the job of copywriter in an advertising agency, you might talk about wanting to be an account manager, working with clients, improving their business, and directing a team. Be careful about naming a job that is completely unrelated, such as being an African safari guide. |

Martin's Interviewing Questions[a] (Continued)

| Martin's Questions | My Suggestions for Answering the Questions |
|---|---|
| **8. What job in our company would you choose if you were given a choice?** | Who knows why interviewers ask nervous people to answer these kinds of questions, but be prepared. Do not name the job you are interviewing for, because you may be seen as having no ambition. If you are interviewing for a job as market analyst, you might say you would like to be vice president of marketing. Be prepared to explain why it interests you. "I love the challenge of finding a unique niche in the market, evaluating competition, and beating it. It is a dynamic job, since the marketplace changes almost daily." |
| **9. What job in our organization do you want to work toward?** | Your answer about what job to aim for might be the same as in the previous question. You will probably not be asked both questions. |

Martin's Interviewing Questions[a] (Continued)

| Martin's Questions | My Suggestions for Answering the Questions |
|---|---|
| **10. What jobs have you enjoyed the most? The least?** | Think about all the jobs you've had, even paper routes and volunteer work. The interviewer is looking for qualities like initiative and leadership. Some things to point out are: the challenge of meeting deadlines, overcoming obstacles to accomplish results, making decisions with limited knowledge and then working to make them the right decisions, and uncovering the true needs of the customer. Topics you should generally avoid are: completing a long list of duties, perfecting someone else's work, or making sure every last cent was accounted for each day. The jobs you liked least will be toughest to explain. Maybe you didn't like a job because you never had any impact on the final outcome, so your job seemed extraneous to the process. Maybe you became frustrated because goals were changed frequently, and you never had a chance to accomplish your goals before they were changed again. Avoid talking about personality conflicts or the politics of the office. Everyone has such conflicts, but talking about them may give the impression that you have a problem working with others. Don't say you hated having a paper route because you had to get up early. |

Martin's Interviewing Questions[a] (Continued)

| Martin's Questions | My Suggestions for Answering the Questions |
| --- | --- |
| **11. Do you prefer a large or small organization? Why?** | There are advantages and disadvantages to each type. Small organizations often require more versatility from each employee, with the result that everyone feels like an important member of the team. At smaller organizations employees typically have less red tape to go through to accomplish their goals, allowing them to make decisions more quickly. Larger organizations usually offer more opportunities for employees to advance or change departments. They are more likely to have the resources necessary to accomplish their goals. If you interview for a small organization, stress the advantages of small companies, but don't overdo it. They may be planning to expand. Many large companies pride themselves on operating like small organizations, so be careful not to emphasize your dislike of small companies. You might want to say that the job always comes down to the people you work with directly, no matter how large the organization. Do not make a career decision based on the size of the company. Anyone who has worked for companies of various sizes can tell you that you can have good and bad experiences in both. |

Martin's Interviewing Questions[a] (Continued)

| Martin's Questions | My Suggestions for Answering the Questions |
|---|---|
| **12. What was your best subject in school? Your worst? Your favorite?** | The more recent your school experiences, the easier this may be for you. Give some reasons for preferring a subject. An acceptable explanation is that you liked a certain subject because the teacher motivated you and helped you appreciate it. Your reasons may be more important than the subject itself: "Science lab allowed me to work with several people to explore untested theories." The interviewer wants to determine your strengths and preferences. Try to put yourself in the best light for the job at hand. |
| **13. Do you know anyone who has ever done the type of work under discussion?** | So often we claim to be interested in a job but don't really know what it involves. If you don't know anyone who has done this job, try to think of someone with similar work experience. At this point, ask more about the job to help you think of someone. Think of your own work. If it's a management job, have you done anything that required similar skills? Maybe you had to juggle several projects at once or you had to get co-workers to cooperate on a job. It is okay to say, "No, I don't know anyone who has had this title, but it sure sounds exciting to me." |

Martin's Interviewing Questions[a] (Continued)

| Martin's Questions | My Suggestions for Answering the Questions |
|---|---|
| **14. Why do you want to work for our organization? How did you happen to apply here?** | If someone referred you, say so and name the person, unless you were asked not to do so. This is also the time to draw on what you learned about the company before the interview: "I understand you are a growing company with an exciting future," or "A solid firm like this offers an opportunity to grow professionally and contribute to long-term goals." Say that you looked into the company: "I applied here because I found your ad in the paper. After reading about your company, I decided I would like to investigate further." If you talked to anyone about the company, you might say, "From the people I have talked to, I believe I would fit in with the team you have on board and have much to contribute." |

Martin's Interviewing Questions[a] (Continued)

| Martin's Questions | My Suggestions for Answering the Questions |
|---|---|
| **15. What are your goals? Long range? Short range?** | No one will remember what you said five years from now, but have them ready now. "I would like to be chief copywriter within five years and lead a marketing team within 10 years." Your plans should include at least a couple of promotions in the first five years. An exception is a sales job on straight commission, since you can increase your income without a promotion. In that case, you should have specific income goals. "I want to be earning $100,000 a year five years from now and $200,000 in 10 years." State your career goals as plans that depend on you, not on someone else deciding whether to promote you. Generally, your goals should be realistic and possible within the confines of the company you interview with. "I want to move from inventory control to production control to marketing, and eventually become a product manager." |

Martin's Interviewing Questions[a] (Continued)

| Martin's Questions | My Suggestions for Answering the Questions |
| --- | --- |
| **16. Will you tell me something about yourself?** | Do not say, "I like people." Also avoid a chronological autobiography, which may lead you to disclose things about yourself that you don't want to say. Try something like this: "I am an enthusiastic, goal-oriented person. I am well-organized, and once I am involved in a project, I become thoroughly committed to seeing it to completion. I love a challenge and get excited about working as a member of a team." Notice that this statement says nothing about your experience in administration. Then try to steer the conversation back to the job by asking: "What qualities are you looking for in a person to fill this position?" Ask about qualities, not experience. |
| **17. What are your strengths? Your weaknesses?** | Do not give your strengths as following instructions well or being punctual. Instead say, "I am a good listener, and I can communicate my ideas well," or "I can usually find several ways to get the same thing accomplished." The challenge, of course, is talking about your weaknesses. Try to make your weakness work for you, not against you. That's what the other applicants are doing. A good response might be, "I become so engrossed in a project, I almost get tunnel vision until I am finished." This is far better than saying, "I tend to lose my temper." |

**Martin's Interviewing Questions[a] (Continued)**

| Martin's Questions | My Suggestions for Answering the Questions |
|---|---|
| **18. Describe a crisis you had to deal with and tell me how you coped with it.** | This is an especially good question to think about ahead of time, since you may draw a blank if taken by surprise. Describe how you dealt with a crisis and what you learned from it. Would you deal with it the same way now? The more life experience you have, the easier you may find this question. The interviewer wants to determine how you deal with crisis situations, since these come up on a regular basis in business. If a minor crisis is the only thing you can think of, preface your answer by saying, "This was a relatively minor incident, but it sure seemed to be a crisis at the time." Don't be afraid to talk about what you would do differently if you had to face the same crisis again. All of us learn from mistakes. |
| **19. What kinds of contributions could you make to our company?** | This question gets at why you are here. Talk about any experience you have in terms of your contribution. If you have no direct experience, play up the fact that you can bring an objective approach to the position. Problems in organizations are more similar than different. Whatever experience you have can help solve problems elsewhere. "I will contribute my ability to remain focused on the goal and motivate others to do the same." |

Martin's Interviewing Questions[a] (Continued)

| Martin's Questions | My Suggestions for Answering the Questions |
|---|---|
| **20. Why are you leaving your present employer?** | Be careful not to say anything negative about your current boss or company, no matter how justified. Use positive statements to explain your move. For example, you are looking for a new opportunity that does not exist where you currently work, or there is no room for advancement. It can make you appear more valuable if you say that you don't necessarily want to leave your current employer. You are just exploring other possibilities, and this one sounded interesting. If you are not asked why you are leaving, don't volunteer it. |
| **21. What is there about you that qualifies you for this position?** | From the interview, determine the kind of person the company seeks and talk about some aspect of yourself that fits well. Use strong, enthusiastic language to help make yourself stand out among the applicants. Don't talk about having an advantage, talk about having a tremendous advantage. Don't speak of being capable, speak of being strong. You might say, "My training as a classroom teacher has taught me how and why people learn, a powerful tool when applied to corporate training. All the technical expertise in the world is not taught unless someone else learns it." This helps you stand out more than saying, "I have been teaching people for years and believe I can transfer these skills to your company." |

Martin's Interviewing Questions[a] (Continued)

| Martin's Questions | My Suggestions for Answering the Questions |
|---|---|
| **22. In what ways did your education prepare you for this job?** | If your educational background is unrelated to the job, talk about what you have learned about human nature and how groups of people act and react. Maybe you have learned to look at all sides of an issue. College is, if nothing else, an exercise in self-discipline. Calling yourself a well-rounded person probably won't explain it. Talk about any education or training you have received and how it applies directly to the job as you know it. Don't hesitate to talk about your education in life's experiences. We all learn lessons from our experiences, especially the difficult ones. Prepare an answer giving a clear example of the wisdom you have gained over the years. Try to be as specific as possible. |
| **23. How would you evaluate your performance on your present job?** | Obviously, put yourself in a good light. Quantify your answers as much as possible, even if you talk about your part in a team effort. "Our department has increased our efficiency by 20% in the past year. Many of the innovations were my suggestions." "Changes in work flow have saved our company $200,000 in the past six months. I implemented those changes." Don't say you think you are good, say that you are good. Don't say you believe you are capable, say you know you are capable. Maybe you are thinking your boss would dispute you, but he's not here. |

Martin's Interviewing Questions[a] (Continued)

| Martin's Questions | My Suggestions for Answering the Questions |
|---|---|
| **24. Are you free to travel? To relocate? Do you have your own transportation?** | These are three distinct questions. If asked together, give separate answers.<br><br>Before answering the question on travel, ask how much travel is expected. Almost no one is willing to spend five nights a week in hotel rooms. Ask how often you would expected to travel, and how long you would be gone at a time. Answer the question in terms of your willingness to travel, not whether you are free to do so. Ideally, the interviewer will not know your marital status or whether you have children. "I have decided that about 60 nights a year is the maximum I am willing to look at the walls of a hotel room, so this job falls well within my limits."<br><br>The question of relocation comes up far more often in interviews than in real life. The interviewer may think the ideal candidate should be available for any promotion or change, anywhere. Whether you are that person or you never want to move from your current location, say you would be open to any relocation if the position were right. There are several reasons to give this answer.<br><br>First, the subject may never come up after you are hired. You will probably not be offered positions in other cities, or you may find equally good opportunities where you are. |

Martin's Interviewing Questions[a] (Continued)

| Martin's Questions | My Suggestions for Answering the Questions |
|---|---|
| **24. Are you free to travel? To relocate? Do you have your own transportation? (Continued)** | Secondly, even if relocation is currently out of the question, you may change your mind, or your circumstances may change. You will never be held to this answer. No one will come to you in five years with a transcript of the interview and force you to move. If you appear too rigid now, you can talk yourself out of an offer. If the company you are interviewing with requires you to relocate five years from now, you can quit and go to another company, but with five more years of experience. You don't want to lose a job over this issue.<br><br>An exception to this is a case when relocation within a specific time period is part of the employment agreement. Do not accept this kind of position if you are unwilling to move.<br><br>On the transportation question, if you currently take the bus or subway to work, say so. Perhaps this new position will allow you to purchase your own car. You might say, "I use public transportation now, which I find easy and always reliable. If I need a car, or decide I want a car, I will purchase one." If the job clearly requires that you have your own transportation, you can say you are currently in the market for an automobile. Don't talk about relying on friends or co-workers to get you to work, even if it is true. It won't do to say, "My neighbor is always home and doesn't mind taking me to work." |

Martin's Interviewing Questions[a] (Continued)

| Martin's Questions | My Suggestions for Answering the Questions |
|---|---|
| **25. In what way is your previous experience applicable to the job for which you are applying?** | The tasks may be completely different, but the skills to complete them may be similar. Concentrate on the skills, and remember you will learn a lot after you get the job. Perhaps you now have a lot of responsibility for the performance of others, but no authority over them – not an uncommon situation. If you need to convince people to complete tasks on time when they don't work for you, think what you could accomplish if you had official authority over them! You may now juggle many projects with different deadlines and constantly changing priorities. You may have to appease those whose priorities get put aside. You may already know how to set a goal and work toward it, no matter how many people or obstacles get in your way. This is much different from talking about tasks. |
| **26. What do you think of your current management? (Or, how are they to work for over at X Company?)** | Do not disparage your current employer. Maybe this is a test of your good taste and professionalism. "My company hires outstanding people who are dedicated to their work. I am ready to make a change and find that currently there are no opportunities for me there." Depending on the interviewer, you might say, "I am an excellent secretary, but I am afraid it is hard for them to see me as anything else. I believe a fresh start is important for me right now." |

Martin's Interviewing Questions[a] (Continued)

| Martin's Questions | My Suggestions for Answering the Questions |
|---|---|
| **27. Why do you think this job will be better than the one you have?** | Depending on the interviewer, you might be able to mention leaving a female career path for a male career path. Don't say you believe there will be fewer problems or less frustration. "In my current job, I am closely supervised, I have no authority to determine how to accomplish even the smallest detail. In this job, I would work more independently, measured more on the end result than the tasks involved." It is okay to say, "Much of my day will probably be the same. I expect that I will have too much to do and will constantly need to define and redefine priorities. The difference is that this job will allow me to impact the bottom line more directly." |
| **28. Whom do you envy? Whom do you admire?** | Try to be prepared for this one. It could stump you otherwise. It has been said that women have few role models or heroines. You do not need to name a woman, but naming someone in business or politics would probably gain more points than naming a movie star. You don't need to name someone the interviewer has ever heard of – maybe you admire your mother. Be sure to explain your reasons for envying or admiring someone. |

Martin's Interviewing Questions[a] (Continued)

| Martin's Questions | My Suggestions for Answering the Questions |
| --- | --- |
| **29. What kind of supervisor do you like best—one who spells things out or a delegator?** | Do not say, "I like to know exactly what is expected of me." This may sound efficient, but it makes you appear unable to make decisions on your own. A good response would be: "I prefer to work for a delegator, because that person is usually more interested in the end result and allows people to accomplish their goals in their own way." Mature people are expected to adjust to their boss's style, so don't carry on and on about what you don't like in a manager. |
| **30. If you had to describe yourself to another person, how would you do it?** | Keep it business, and talk in terms of working: "I would say that I am an ethical person who enjoys working on a worthwhile project. I am reasonable when dealing with others as a team member. I get very excited about my work" You may be asked what you do for recreation. Most employers want well-rounded people who enjoy play as well as work. If you are involved in community service of some kind, mention it. If asked, talk about any sports or activities you enjoy. If you have a family, it may be hard not to discuss them, but keep them completely out of the interview. |

Martin's Interviewing Questions[a] (Continued)

| Martin's Questions | My Suggestions for Answering the Questions |
| --- | --- |
| **31. Have you any experience in this kind of work?** | Don't panic. It is only a question, just like all the others. You wouldn't be here if they weren't at least partially interested in hiring you. Remember the next person they interview may be someone who believes he is qualified when he has only 40% of the knowledge and skills needed. Don't start your sentences with a negative, "I've never been a line supervisor, but..." Find a skill that relates to the job and discuss it. "I have developed the ability to remain focused on the outcome, adjusting the process where necessary," is better than, "I want to get the job done right. I don't let others' deadlines compromise my quality." You may be asked outright about your direct experience for this job: "Have you ever supervised part of an assembly line?" Your response could be, "No, I haven't. But I am interested in the job and learn quickly. Have you ever hired someone for this position who had no direct experience? How did that person work out?" Your composure in answering this question can sell you. |

Martin's Interviewing Questions[a] (Continued)

| Martin's Questions | My Suggestions for Answering the Questions |
|---|---|
| **32. How did you happen to choose this particular field of work?** | If you have worked in this field, discuss how you happened to start. Most people did not make a conscious decision to enter their field of work. They got a job, it led to something else, and they eventually found themselves in a certain field for an extended period of time. If this is your story, explain that while you may not have chosen this field, you enjoy it and want to remain. If you haven't previously worked in this area and you want this job, point out that you are choosing this field and why. |
| **33. What about our product or service is of interest to you?** | Talk about the benefits of a product or service to the company's customers. There are companies out there who don't care about serving their customers; but you don't want to work for any of them. If you have read enough ahead of time, you might say, "The application of ferrous metal to polypropylene can reduce downtime by 30%. Downtime in a factory means wages, overhead, a backlog of orders, and shipping problems. How could I not be excited about a product that can help solve this problem?" You don't have to understand how it all works. In a high-tech company, no one understands how everything works. You don't have to benefit from a product directly to become enthused about it. |

Martin's Interviewing Questions[a] (Continued)

| Martin's Questions | My Suggestions for Answering the Questions |
|---|---|
| **34. Would you guess our margin of profit to be large? Small? Explain.** | In some industries, a 3% profit margin is considered excellent. In others, 30% is considered average. Remember the definitions of industry and profit margin. The most recent quarterly report or the annual report will give you this information, or enough information to calculate it. If the company is privately held, you will not have this information. "I know you have an excellent product line, and if you are successfully controlling costs, your profit margin is well within the industry average." If you know they are currently writing off an unprofitable subsidiary, or something else unusual is affecting their profit margin, mention it. You won't get the job by saying, "Gosh, you mean you only make 2%?" |
| **35. What are the advantages of work in your chosen field? The disadvantages?** | "There is nothing like shipping that difficult order, which you thought you would never get out on time, to give you a real sense of accomplishment. All the disadvantages – problems with retooling, snags in production, trucking strikes, and everything else – seem unimportant when the customer finally gets the order." In this case, you have incorporated the advantages and disadvantages into one sentence. Another approach to talking about disadvantages is: "The disadvantages of business are often the same for every field: different groups of people with different agendas and different priorities trying to work together." |

Martin's Interviewing Questions[a] (Continued)

| Martin's Questions | My Suggestions for Answering the Questions |
|---|---|
| **36. Where do you see yourself in this company five years from now? Ten years?** | This is similar to the question about goals, but prepare yourself for both questions. Talk as if you are there to stay. "In five years I want to be a product manager. In 10 years I would like to be plant manager." "I want to learn the product line on the sales desk and move into outside sales. In 10 years, I want to be a sales manager." Know where you *can* go from this job, even if you have no desire to move on. Get an organizational chart. Draw on your own experience. If you want to change departments, say so. "Drafting is an important step. From there I want to move into technical writing and eventually to marketing." Try to make your plan sound like a reasonable progression. Don't sell yourself short. Whatever you do, don't say, "Gosh, I don't know where I want to go from here. I suppose I will learn more about your company and will be promoted according to my performance." If you're even *tempted* to say that, read this book again. |

a. Copyright © 1987 by Phyllis Martin
From MARTIN'S MAGIC FORMULA FOR GETTING THE RIGHT JOB By Phyllis Martin Reprinted by permission of St. Martin's Press Incorporated

While these questions are fairly inclusive, you may still be asked a question that really throws you off. Remember to avoid panic during the interview. You might need some time to think about an answer. "I will drop you a line tomorrow with that answer. I would like to think that through more thoroughly."

## *How Much Will They Pay You?*

It is best to leave the topic of pay until late in the interview process, if possible. If you are asked about it early, you might say, "I would like to know more about the position before we discuss a specific salary." Actually, you want them to be convinced you are the candidate of choice.

We are expected to negotiate for income. This is a new one for most women. We want to take what is offered without all that fuss, and we don't want to make someone mad when we don't even work for them yet. By now you should realize that there is usually no set pay for certain jobs. There is usually a range, and the range may be as much as $20,000 from bottom to top. You want to get as close to the top of the range as you can. Don't think that you should start near the bottom because you are new. Newer people often make more than employees with more seniority, because they are perceived as demanding more.

There are several different philosophies on how to handle this negotiation. Try to keep them in mind, and do what seems most appropriate under the circumstances. All raises, and to a certain extent all future offerings, will be based on your initial salary. Don't let this paralyze you, but remember that salary is almost always a negotiable topic. Even if it is not, it will be to your advantage to attempt to negotiate. You will be seen as assertive and more valuable in the eyes of the employer.

*The Occupational Outlook Handbook* and the *Dictionary of Occupational Titles*, which should be available at a library, may help you determine the salary range for a job. Be sure to set some salary boundaries of your own before the interview. Chastain explains that on the whole, women seem to have lower salary aspirations than men. Try to raise your aspirations and negotiate for more. Otherwise, you will have to settle for less.

An employer will usually try to base your pay on what you currently make or what you made on your last job. You will be asked about your current salary. Be careful how you answer this one. If you have health insurance and other benefits provided, your employer pays approximately 35-40% of your salary for them. Include this 35-40% in the "package" you discuss. Any bonuses or commissions should also be included. You might also say, "I expect a raise soon, and my compensation package will be $35,000 by the end of the year." Now is the time to explain that you are looking to change positions because you believe you deserve to earn more.

If an employment agent has gotten you the interview, that person may know the salary range that the employer has in mind. This person may or may not be prepared to negotiate hard for you. Prepare to negotiate for yourself.

If you are asked directly what kind of salary you expect, you can name a figure. Make it higher than you are willing to accept. Say something like, "I believe my contributions should be worth about $50,000 annually. How does that sound to you?" Another approach is to throw a question back at the interviewer: "What is the salary range for this position?"

Don't assume that companies want the cheapest candidate they can get. Sure, they want to contain costs, but they also want to maximize profits, and they know they have to invest to do it. Don't think that your willingness to work for less money will make you the most desirable candidate. If we put a low price on ourselves, what can we expect others to do?

Continue salary negotiations as you would other negotiations. If you are interested in the job but simply cannot accept their offer, suggest an increase in your pay after you have had a chance to prove your worth, in three or six months, for example. A bonus might be easier for the company to deliver than a raise, and it could be a bargaining chip for you.

## *Bill and Jane*

Let's suppose that you are interviewing candidates for a position in the marketing research department of a corporation. People in this position often move on to the development of company brochures and other literature. They work closely with the advertising and sales departments, and sometimes they take a job in one of those departments. While the position is considered an entry-level job in your corporation, you are encouraged to get college-educated or experienced candidates because some of your top-level executives began here. It is considered an important job, and good training ground for further opportunity in the company. You have two candidates to interview today, Bill and Jane. You are a man, but you like to consider yourself progressive on the issue of equal opportunities for women. In fact, you would like to see your team more balanced, and the majority of people currently in this position are men.

Bill comes in first. He is 25, has a B.A. degree in English, and has been working for the last two years since graduating from college. He has been a telemarketer for a home-improvement company, making appointments for the salesmen. He is dressed in an inexpensive but well-fitting suit, and his shoes are polished. He seems confident enough. To begin the interview, you briefly explain the job responsibilities and career advancement possibilities. You ask Bill if he thinks he would be good at the job and why.

***Bill:*** I have a lot of experience calling on people I don't know. I know how to get people to talk to get the information I need, you know. If you need to know where your market is, or who your best customers are, just let me at them, and I'll find the information for you. I believe I should be considered for management at some point in the future, you know. I was the president of my fraternity in my senior year and was very successful at getting the guys to do what needed to be done in the best interest of all concerned.

As the interviewer, you find Bill a bit exuberant, but you chalk it up to youth. He is certainly interested. You ask him about his five- and 10-year career goals.

***Bill:*** In five years, I would like to have been promoted from this position into a spot that takes full advantage of my creative capacity. I've watched the guys in design and advertising come up with promos and the like. I know I could do that, and that I would be really good at it. This job would give me a real feel for what the customers are like and what they need, so that the advertising and public relations work could be customer-oriented. By 10 years from now, I'll be middle-aged, and I expect to be a vice president, or at least assistant vice president. I have strong leadership qualities, and a good work ethic, you know. I think I could really be an asset to you.

Next you interview Jane. She is 35 – middle-aged, according to Bill – and has been home taking care of her family for the last eight years. Prior to that, she worked as an assistant to the owner of a small electronics distributor. She is well-groomed and seems confident enough. You begin the interview by outlining the responsibilities of the job. (Note: you neglect to point out the advancement opportunities, as you did with Bill.

You may not be quite as enlightened as you thought.) You ask Jane if she would be interested in the job and why.

> ***Jane:*** I think I would really like this job. It would give me a chance to learn about your line of work and talk to a lot of different people about their needs. I enjoy talking to people. I am a hard worker and am not afraid to try new things.

As the interviewer, you are impressed with the way Jane presents herself. She is poised and more articulate than Bill. Maturity means a lot in any job. However, she has given you no reason why hiring her would be good for you, only her own reasons for wanting the job. You ask her about her five- and 10-year career goals.

> ***Jane:*** Gosh, I haven't thought about that much. This job sounds really interesting. I believe I can learn to do it well, and I hope to be promoted when the time comes. I don't really want to be president of the company or anything, but I am anxious to do my part to make the company a success.

Both these people want the job, and they both could probably learn to do the job. But Bill has given you specific examples of what he hopes to accomplish – getting to know customers and finding out their needs – and why – to make marketing and advertising customer-oriented. He seems pretty naive about the future, expecting to be a vice president within 10 years, but he definitely has ambition. Jane hopes to be promoted "when the time comes." She gives no indication of her future aspirations. As a matter of fact, she plays down any ambition by stating that she doesn't want to be president of the company.

This scenario is an oversimplification, but it is neither inaccurate nor very unusual. Bill has overrated his experience and capabilities, while Jane has underrated hers, or at least failed to elaborate enough. As an interviewer, you listen to people overrate themselves all day long. While Jane may seem like a breath of fresh air, she appears to have no direction, no goals for herself. Like many interviewers, you are a man. You are not aware of the body of training that has caused Jane to give the answers she has. You only know how she presents herself in comparison to others, who seem to know more about how to interview.

So how could Jane have done better? She should have talked about how she could contribute to the company, rather than what she personally would gain from the job. She could have pulled from her experiences (she has lived 10 years longer than Bill) to highlight her strengths. Maybe she has led a group of volunteers or organized a fund-raiser. Maybe she wrote the brochure for her child's preschool. Phrases like *hard worker* and *like people* don't really mean much; anyone can say them. She could have described how she has worked toward specific goals. She could have given the interviewer a better idea of what she meant by not being afraid to try new things.

Jane should have had some five- and 10-year career goals ready to discuss. Since the interviewer did not describe advancement opportunities, she should have asked about them. Jane could have asked how the job was measured and what standard of performance was considered exceptional. In this case, Jane started out with some advantages. The interviewer would have preferred to find a qualified woman, and she was more mature than her exuberant counterpart. However, as the interview progressed, she lost her advantage. Bill would probably be given the position, and Jane would be told they had found someone more qualified. Jane would assume they hired someone with direct experience.

## *Once it's Over*

Never walk out of any interview without an agreed-upon next step. Find out whom the next interview will be with, and when. Find out when a decision will be made, and try to find out the criteria to be used in the decision. Express your interest in the job. Say something like, "I believe I could contribute a great deal to your company and would like to be considered for this position." Even if you are unsure of your interest, express interest. Our first reaction to a job may not be accurate.

Find out what they think of you. "Do you think I could do the job?" "Do you have any hesitation about considering me for the position?" "Do you believe I will be back for another interview?" "What do you think of me?" If the response is, "Well, we have several applicants and we will be interviewing for a couple of weeks yet," don't accept it. "What kinds of criteria will be used in making your hiring decision?" Try not to leave an interview with no idea of how successful you were. Ask what the next step is, what you need to do, and what you can expect from them.

Go home and write the interviewer. Thank the interviewer for taking the time and express your interest in the job. Remind the interviewer of why you would be good for the position.

It is not uncommon for an interviewer to say, "Don't call us, we'll call you." If you are told you will hear by Thursday and you do not, call the employer Friday morning. Express your interest in the position, and ask whether a decision has been made. Do not be surprised if the whole process drags on longer than anticipated. If you are rejected, take the opportunity to find out how you could have interviewed more effectively. Ask the employer where else you might apply.

Let's say you are offered a job you are interested in. It is not always wise to accept a job on the spot. Sometimes there is a lot of hype in an interview and once you think about it, you may change your mind. It is usually reasonable to say that you would like a day or two to think about it. Do not say that you want to discuss it with your husband or boyfriend. Occasionally, the company may need an answer right away. If you are unsure, ask if they will leave the offer open for at least several hours: "This is an important decision for me. Could I get back to you this afternoon? How about 3:00?" Of course, if you know you want the job, and the price is right, accept.

## *Keep At It*

The process of job hunting is a humbling experience. All successful people have been turned down from jobs they wanted badly. See every interview as a vote of confidence in your abilities and a chance to hone your interviewing skills. There is a job out there for you. Keep trying until you land it.

***"Almost always, men and women who follow male career paths in private industry will make considerably more money than those who follow female career paths. Over the course of a lifetime, the difference in pay is staggering." -Patricia Smith***

# Epilogue

Business is just a bunch of people doing their jobs. Some jobs pay more than others. If you decide to change lanes to switch to a male career path, the initial switch will be the hardest part, but you have done hard things before. It might take longer than you hoped, but you will be moving in the right direction.

1. Change your style of clothing. Wear tailored, dark suits and low pumps to work every day.
2. Forget about whether you are a *career woman* or not. You are you, and you have magnificent things to offer. At the same time, be aware of this distinction in the minds of others and use it to your advantage.
3. Work on your confidence level. Surround yourself with positive people whenever you can. Hold your head high and fake it until you start to believe it.

4. Begin to evaluate your approach and your reactions to situations. Determine your commitment to teamwork, your approach to risk, your balance between perfection and timeliness. Adjust your behavior where necessary.
5. Get used to moving forward when you are not completely sure of what you're doing or what the outcome may be. Trust your judgment and your ability to make the right decision or make it right after it's been made.
6. Become aware of the negotiations going on around you and learn to participate.
7. Start to become more results-oriented. Determine the bottom line in various situations and work toward that end.
8. Draft, write, and rewrite a resume.
9. Become more aware of the opportunities around you. Begin to seek new opportunities. Let your career be defined by no one but you.
10. Expect disappointments, setbacks, and outright resistance. It's all part of the process.
11. Take charge. Move forward. My thoughts and prayers are with you.

## *Bibliography*

Asher, Donald. (1991). *The Overnight Resume.* Berkeley, CA: Ten Speed Press.

Bryant, Gay, with Editors of Working Woman. (1984). *The Working Woman Report: Succeeding in Business in the '80's.* New York: Simon & Schuster.

Chastain, Sherry. (1980). *Winning the Salary Game: Salary Negotiations for Women.* New York: John Wiley & Sons, Inc.

Coxford, Lola. (1989). *Resume Writing Made Easy.* Scottsdale, AZ: Gorsuch Scarisbrick

Dight, Janet. (1986). *Breaking the Secretary Barrier: How to Get Out From Behind the Typewriter and into a Management Job.* New York: McGraw Hill.

Friedman, Martha. (1988). *Overcoming the Fear of Success.* New York: Warner Books.

Halas, Celia. (1986). *Why Can't a Woman be More Like a Man? The 20 Questions Men Ask Most Frequently About Women.* New York: Macmillan.

Harragan, Betty Lehan. (1977). *Games Mother Never Taught You: Corporate Gamesmanship for Women.* New York: Warner Books.

Krannich, Ronald & Banis, William (1991). *The Overnight Resume.* Berkeley, CA: Ten Speed Press.

Lainson, Suzanne. (1985). *Crash Course, the Instant MBA.* New York: Putnam Publishing Group, The Stonesong Press, Inc.

Martin, Phyllis. (1987). *Martin's Magic Formula for Getting the Right Job.* New York: St. Martin's Press.

Melia, Jinx & Lyttle, Pauline. (1986). *Why Jenny Can't Lead: Understanding the Male Dominant System.* Grand Junction, CO: Operational Politics Inc.

Molloy, John T. (1988). *New Dress for Success*, revised edition of *Dress for Success*, 1975. New York: Warner Books.

Moore, Lynda. (1986). *Not as Far as You Think: The Realities of Working Women*. Lexintong, MA: Lexington Books.

Schaef, Anne Wilson. (1985). Women's Reality: *An Emerging Female System in a White Male Society*. San Francisco, CA: Perennial Library: Harper & Row.

Schwartz, David. (1987). *The Magic of Thinking Big*. New York: Simon & Schuster.

Shainess, Natalie. (1984). *Sweet Suffering: Woman as Victim.* Indianapolis, IN: BobbsMerrill.

Wyse, Lois. (1983). *The Six-Figure Woman, and How to Be On*e. New York: Linden Press; Simon & Schuster.